A Practical

Pro

Planning

For all those who have known the pain of change and the joy of discovery.

> Your plan is not a crystal ball.
> It is the framework within which
> you coordinate work and test the
> impact of changes.

A Practical Guide to

Project Planning

Celia Burton
With Norma Michael

Kogan Page Ltd, London
Nichols Publishing Company,
New Jersey

First published in 1994

Kogan Page Limited
120 Pentoville Road
London N1 9JN

© Celia Burton and Norma Michael, 1994

Published in the United States of America by Nichols Publishing,
PO BOX 6036, East Brunswick, New Jersey 08816

British Library Cataloguing in Publication Data
A CIP record for this book is available from the British Library.

ISBN (UK) 07494 1116 3

Library of Congress Cataloging-in-Publication Data
Burton, Celia.
   A practical guide to project planning / by Celia Burton, in collaboration with Norma Michael.
        p. cm.
   Includes bibliographical references and index.
   ISBN 0-89397-396-3 $27.95
   1. Industrial project management. 2. Planning. I. Michael, Norma. II. Title.
HD69.P75B874 1994
658.4 012—dc20   94–25010
                                                              CIP

Typeset by Saxon Graphics Ltd, Derby
Printed in England by Clays Ltd, St Ives plc

Contents

Part 3 – Develop the summary plan (detailed planning)

Part 4 – Implement, amend and review the plan and develop the template

Part 5 – Marketing, problem solving, brainstorming, data modelling

*L*ist of figures

*L*ist of cases

Acknowledgements

We thank all the following for their help: Wendy Rule for reading the first draft, and Chris Comber, John Ahearn, Nick Ashill, Paul Daniel, David Irving, Commander Richard Jackson, Brian Lilley, David Oakes, Chuck Wareham, Vincent Burton, Greg Cottrell, Fiona Bain, Mark Blumsky, Brett Weaver, Brenda Prosser.

Our thanks also to Dr Nigel Piercy for permission to use his marketing planning matrices.

We feel particularly indebted to Philip Mudd and thank him for his support and patience.

Thanks also to: Synergy International Limited, Internet '94, the Cardiff Business School, the Ministry of Defence, Otus Design, Vinvent Ltd, Lilley Management, Victoria University, Mischief Shoes.

*I*ntroduction

Planning hazards are legion. So are planning sceptics. This book shows you how to avoid hazards, and aims to convince readers of the enormous benefits and satisfactions that accrue from using the latest quick and easy planning methods. In today's competitive business world, the ability of a company or person to plan quickly and effectively is a means to gaining the competitive edge.

On the personal level, gone are the days when planners worked in isolation. In the organizations of today and tomorrow, whatever your role in the organization, expect to be involved in planning processes either as part of the project team or as an end user. The planning process, therefore, is something about which everyone in business needs to be informed.

From our initial research into what books were available we found that while there were numerous books on the topics of project management and project planning, most of them talked to the strategists, the people at the top. Our first book, *A Practical Guide to Project Management*, provided guidelines for people at all levels of planning. With those same readers in view this complementary book, *A Practical Guide to Project Planning*, goes deeply into the planning process. It sets out easy-to-follow, futuristic guidelines for both the experienced and the inexperienced, the technical and the non-technical at any level within an organization. Although the main focus is on organizational planning, you can apply the techniques widely, say to personal projects such as getting married, building your own house and planning your world trip!

It may have been your experience that often project planning begins, then breaks down, foundering on the large amount of detail traditional planning engenders. Planners can become so weighed down by detail that they convince themselves and others that the amount of detail is unmanageable and warrants abandonment of the plan.

At other times you may have found that in attempting to deal with the complexities that can occur, some people develop an attitude which summed up is: 'I can't plan because I don't know what's going to happen in the future.' For example, 'I don't know how the legislation's going to change' (or the market, the economy, anything!). Typical excuses for not planning are:

- Situations change even while the plans are being made.
- One person makes the plans and has to pass them on to somebody who either does not understand them or is not committed to them, or both.
- Planning takes too much time, becomes too complex.

'So,' they say, 'we'll just start the project and see how it goes.' This approach guarantees management by crisis, leading to, at best, a poorly executed job and loss of credibility.

Our overall aim has been to provide a practical book written in plain language giving the latest planning techniques. Our secondary aim is to persuade you to use them. Quick and easy planning methods, lots of case histories, and – a picture being worth a thousand words – diagrams and charts, make competent, effective planning accessible to you.

We recommend that you read all of this book before using the planning techniques.

PART 1

*O*VERVIEW OF PRACTICAL PLANNING PROCESS

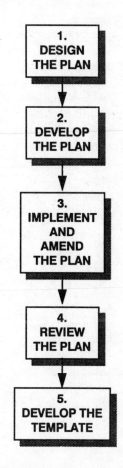

1.
DESIGN
THE PLAN

2.
DEVELOP
THE PLAN

3.
IMPLEMENT
AND
AMEND
THE PLAN

4.
REVIEW
THE PLAN

5.
DEVELOP THE
TEMPLATE

CHAPTER 1 | *T*he basics of project planning

As the part title states, this is an overview. Be confident that the topics mentioned here will be dealt with in detail in the relevant chapters that follow.

PRACTICAL PLANNING PROCESS

Planning begins with an idea which is in response to a perceived need. You could say that the plan is part of the solution to a problem. So, we begin with an idea. From it we design the plan, develop the plan, implement and amend the plan and, at the end of the project, review the plan. Finally, using the amended plan, we can develop a template for future use. As simple as that! Figure 1 sets those steps out for you.

Design the plan and develop the plan (boxes 1 and 2 of Figure 1)

Here you are setting up the project. The design and development of your summary plan are your first steps towards completion of an extended planning document (text supported by diagrams) which sets out:

Figure 1

20

- The outcome that is needed
- Why it is needed
- How you are going to achieve the end result
- The resources you will need.

So, obviously, at the beginning you will need to ask questions such as:

- Where do we need to be?
- Why do we need to be there?
- Where are we now?
- How are we going to get to where we want to be?

These questions will help you to analyse your situation. The answers to these questions become the springboard from which you launch into the full development of your plan. We have set this analytical approach out for you in Figure 2.

During the planning process, continue to analyse all aspects of the needs of the project and its effects both short and long term. The following case illustrates this.

CASE 1 – DREAMCREAM BISCUITS TAKES THE CAKE

Crackerjack Biscuits decides it wants more of the market for a certain type of biscuit that is doing very well for its main competitor, Dreamcream Ltd. When Crackerjack introduces a slightly larger version of the same biscuit in attractive packaging for the same price, it captures the market for that type of biscuit.

Later, looking back, the deprived company, Dreamcream, is forced to ask itself why it took over a year to hit back at Crackerjack and regain the lost market.

The answer is, of course, that in the very beginning the stated outcome of Dreamcream's original planning, to get that biscuit on the supermarket shelves, should not have been the end of the project. If they had addressed the question of what to do if a competitor fought back and edged them out, they would have built into their plan a mechanism for quickly regaining the market. Once they were into forward thinking, not only did they devise a good marketing plan, but from it they developed a template for the future. Now they can respond to market challenges in less than half the time.

■■■■

Right from the start and as your plan progresses, make sure you have approval for what you propose. Get your proposals signed off. Your first sign-off will most likely be approval of the idea which is to form the basis of the project. After that get your 'big picture' plan, that is your summary plan, signed off before you expend resources on detailed planning.

Implement and amend the plan (box 3 of Figure 1)

This is where the work you have planned gets done, and where, using monitoring and control mechanisms, you keep track of what is happening and measure impacts. You develop scenarios to aid decision making. Where necessary, you amend the plan.

Review the plan (box 4 of Figure 1)

Here we think of the future. What have we learned and how would we do it differently to do it better next time? The review generates recommendations and provides an historical record.

Develop the template (box 5 of Figure 1)

Usually templates are developed from the review (above). Templates have proved to be powerful adjuncts to planning. Here are two examples of amazing achievements made possible by the use of templates: one is set in the USA where a toothpaste manufacturer we heard of can change their production line in three hours; even more awe-inspiring, we are told that in Japan one car manufacturer's production line can achieve changeover to a completely new model in two minutes. Needless to say, the use of templates is not restricted to production lines.

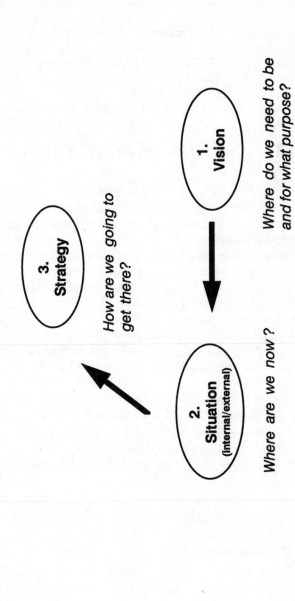

SITUATION ANALYSIS

1.
Vision

Where do we need to be and for what purpose?

3.
Strategy

How are we going to get there?

2.
Situation
(Internal/external)

Where are we now?

Figure 2

CORE FACTORS AND UNIQUE FEATURES

All plans consist of core factors and unique features. Budget, communication (internal and external), resources (human and time) and quality control are the factors common to all projects, namely the 'core' factors. Unique features are the work, structure and strategies that are determined by the specific nature of a project.

PROJECT PLANNING – A POWERFUL MANAGEMENT TOOL

We define 'project' as work that has a beginning and an end, and the satisfactory outcome of a project as a product. A product can be intangible, as in a customer service, or manufactured and as tangible as a toothpaste tube.

Projects mean change. Change requires planning. From the concept to the outcome, practical planning is what makes the change happen. Or not happen, because by enabling you to look ahead, practical planning can warn you off a bad idea early in the piece, allowing you to save face and money. Or planning may steer you in a different direction.

When you plan, you are preparing your case for what you want or need to produce the product. Consider those times when your need is to convince and persuade senior management or a client or your own staff. 'Management don't question my plans any more,' a bank official told us. 'I've built my credibility by showing I can plan and get better than average results.'

From any point of view, planning is a powerful management tool. Ultimately your plan is a potent communication tool for decision making.

TYPES OF PLANS

Your overall plan consists of two main types of plans: the 'big picture' plan (the summary plan) and the 'smaller picture' plans (more detailed than the 'big picture' plan). In varying degrees of detail, the following may become sub-sets of the summary plan.

- **Task plans:** which define what has to be done to complete the project
- **Resource plans:** which define people, materials and equipment required
- **Cost plans:** which define the cost of each task
- **Communication plans:** which define all areas of internal and external communication including when communications are to be sent
- **Time control plans:** which define how long a task should take (due-by dates) and monitor and control actual time taken against the estimated time
- **Quality plans:** which determine standards of quality required and how to meet them.

FROM THE CORPORATE PLAN TO THE PROJECT PLAN

Whatever you are planning, remember that nothing should be planned in isolation. The mission statement of an organization is usually the *fons et origo*, the fountain or beginning from which subsequent planning originates. You may feel you have what is an outstanding idea. Are you sure it meets your company's mission statement and divisional objectives? Do you know your company's mission statement? Does your company have a mission statement? It is important that you understand the larger organizational picture and relate your individual work to it. See your assignment as part of the corporate whole (or 'hole', if you like, into which you may slip if you fail to widen your perspective!).

THE LIVING DOCUMENT

Your completed plan is a document consisting of text and diagrams which presents both the 'big picture' or main plan, which we call the summary plan, and the subsidiary or sub-set plans.

Figuratively speaking you have a map. This map sets out the main route to your destination and the side trips that are essential to your getting there.

Throughout the various stages of the planning process, the plan should be able to accommodate easily to change. Changes may even include revision of the outcome itself. That is why the text of the plan, plus the supporting graphics, form what is known as a 'living document'.

Summary

- The project planning process is the framework within which work is coordinated and impacts tested
- You obtain approval of the plan in the form of sign-offs throughout the planning process
- During the planning process you analyse all aspects of the needs of the project and its effects, both in the long and short term
- All project plans consist of core factors and unique features
- A plan contains a main summary plan and sub-set plans
- Planning is a powerful management tool
- Projects bring about change in the form of products which meet the company mission statement and divisional objectives
- Nothing should be planned in isolation
- The plan is a living document that adapts easily to change during the life of the project.

The following chapters take you through easy, sure-fire planning procedures that use the latest techniques of planning that you can adapt to your own work environment. The idea is to simplify the planning process and allow you to develop plans very quickly. Know-how takes the fear out of planning.

PART 2 | *D*ESIGN THE SUMMARY PLAN

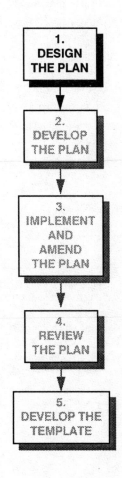

1. DESIGN THE PLAN

2. DEVELOP THE PLAN

3. IMPLEMENT AND AMEND THE PLAN

4. REVIEW THE PLAN

5. DEVELOP THE TEMPLATE

CHAPTER	*T*he whole
2	picture

This chapter describes what you need to do to design your 'big picture' summary plan. Fast track planning techniques using specially designed worksheets enable rapid assessment of what the project requires.

It pays to think big as you begin planning, whether you are planning the whole project or a bit of it. Not 'big' in terms of expenditure of resources particularly – 'big' in the sense of extending your thinking: a) beyond that first perceived vision; b) beyond your own personal involvement in the project if you are one of several project planners. In all planning, stick with the big picture. See the whole. If you are planning chunks of work, see where your bit fits into the whole.

PAINTING THE 'BIG PICTURE' OF THE PROJECT

When you have done what is required to design your 'big picture' summary plan, you will have:

1. Analysed the situation as follows:

- vision identified (where do you want to be?)
- purpose identified (why do you need to be there?)
- current situation identified (where are you now?)
- strategy identified (how are you going to get there, i.e. achieve the vision?).

2. Set out in logical sequence what has to be completed (chunks of work) to achieve the vision

3. Linked and coded each chunk of work.

The following example illustrates how a consultant helped identify the big picture, taking the planners past their own narrow interpretation of what was needed.

Example

Scenario An art gallery where a new exhibition is to be mounted. A planning consultant is brought in. The owners of the gallery have already asked themselves about the purpose of the exhibition and their vision of what would be in place at the end of the planning. They give this information to the consultant.

Purpose To present for the local public's enjoyment an exhibition of paintings, carvings and pottery during its nationwide tour.

Vision 'Exhibition opened'

The consultant challenges the vision. Questions and answers play a very big part in the planning that follows. Using the big picture approach with the art gallery project planning team, the consultant's first question is: 'If the purpose is to present for the local public's enjoyment an exhibition of paintings, carvings and pottery during its nationwide tour, what about managing the exhibition for its duration and dismantling it when it is over?'

Forced to widen their thinking, the project planning team then includes in the summary plan chunks of work that cover:

- Management of the exhibition
- Security during the exhibition
- Dismantling of the exhibits when the exhibition ends.

Now the thinking caps are on. A team member asks, 'What about reviewing the plan and amending it?' Someone suggests making a template for the next touring exhibition. Then there is the budget for the following year. (Based on the evaluation of the exhibition, the budget has to be submitted *within a week of the end of the exhibition.*) Realization begins to grow about all the chunks of work still to be done beyond that first vision of 'exhibition opened'.

Using the 'big picture' approach, the consultant takes the team past their first vision to a much broader vision. Figure 3 sets out in stages the chunks of work necessary beyond the initial vision of 'exhibition opened'. Their summary plan shows this in the form of a logic diagram, a method now widely used in 'big picture' planning. Alphabetical coding appears in Figure 3. Its use and the use of the logic diagram are explained under 'Chunks of work' that follows below. Please note that this is about what you do in designing your plan. *How* you actually do it is covered under the heading 'The method – where and how you plan' in Chapter 3.

In the art gallery example, if the team had not planned beyond that first vision ('exhibition opened') it is possible stress levels would have risen during the exhibition.

But there was also the question of detail. In the consultant's first planning steps she rightly limited the team's thinking to identifying what work (chunks of work) had to be completed to achieve the vision. At this stage she steered them away from details. Details were not part of the big picture – not part of designing the plan, but part of the next stage, developing it. Considering details then would have been counterproductive, holding them up, taking them off the fast track, bogging them down in a mass of information not yet relevant.

CHUNKS OF WORK, THE LOGIC DIAGRAM, CODING AND MILESTONES

During a brainstorming session, you:

- Define the objective which is the final output of your project and any impacts it is likely to create
- Brainstorm for chunks of work that will have to be completed to achieve the desired objective.

At first, do not worry about what order the chunks come in (see Figure 4). At the end of the brainstorming arrange them in logical order, i.e. set them out in the order in which they must be

SUMMARY PLAN – EXHIBITION PROJECT EXAMPLE *(shown in logic diagram format)*

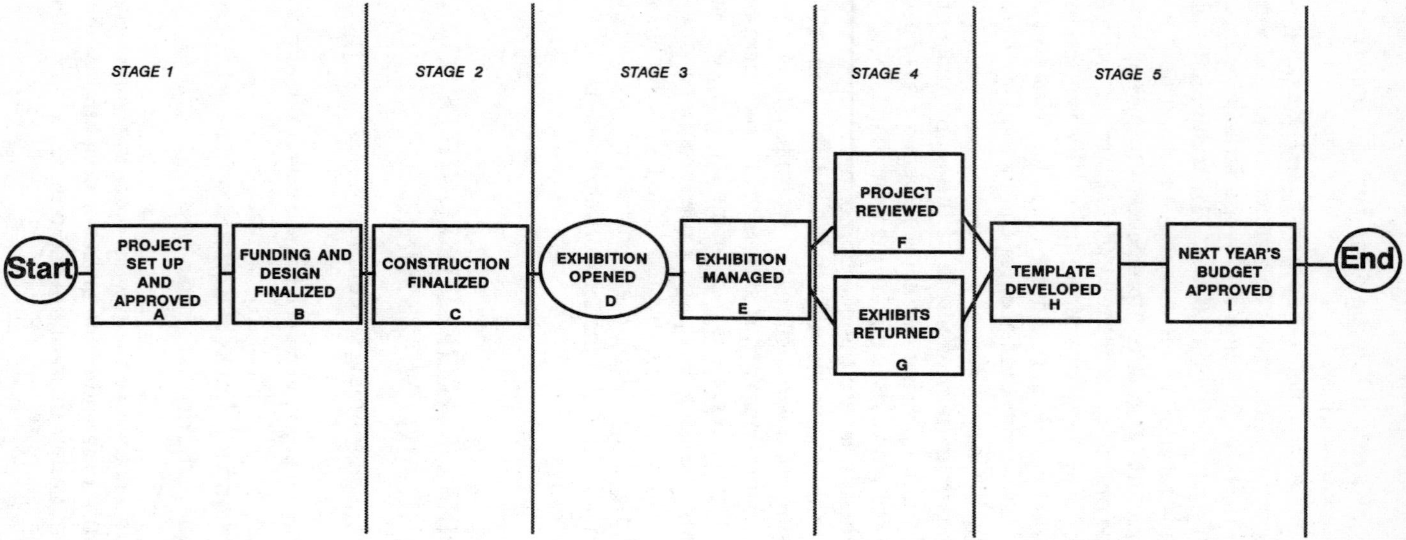

Figure 3

32

SUMMARY PLAN – CHUNKS OF WORK IDENTIFIED

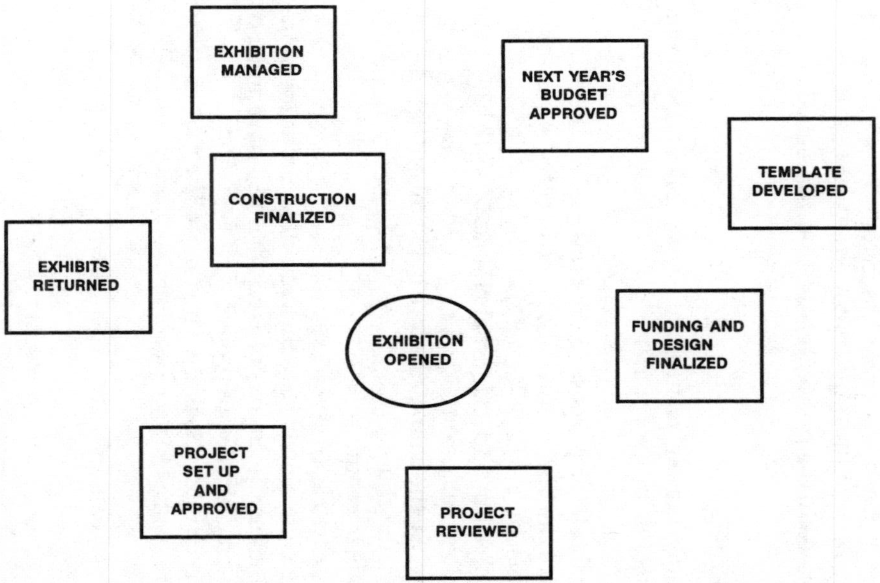

TEMPLATE DEVELOPED

FUNDING AND DESIGN FINALIZED

NEXT YEAR'S BUDGET APPROVED

PROJECT REVIEWED

EXHIBITION OPENED

CONSTRUCTION FINALIZED

EXHIBITION MANAGED

PROJECT SET UP AND APPROVED

EXHIBITS RETURNED

Figure 4

done before the next work can begin. Code and link them (Figure 5). This becomes your summary plan logic diagram. Later, the code will link chunks to the lower level detail plans – especially useful when you are using computers.

To digress for a moment; when you are working on the detailed developing of your plan, you will revisit the summary plan because much of the time you may have to review and amend your first cut of the summary plan.

Another point; some project planners see each completed chunk of work as a project milestone, that is, a major event in the project. Milestones, like chunks of work, are typically expressed in the past tense, e.g. 'Contract signed'.

Summary

Painting the big picture is very simple and straightforward. During this process you:

● Establish the purpose of the project
● State the vision of what will be in place at the end of the project
● Brainstorm or decide what chunks of work have to be done to realize that vision
● Arrange the chunks of work in logical order
● Link the chunks
● Code the chunks.

At the end you will have the logic diagram, as mentioned above. It identifies the chunks of work that will have to be completed during the life of your project.

This chapter sets out what you do. The next chapter tells you how to do it.

SUMMARY PLAN – CHUNKS OF WORK ARRANGED IN LOGICAL ORDER AND CODED

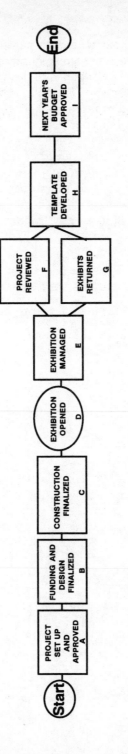

Start

| PROJECT SET UP AND APPROVED A | FUNDING AND DESIGN FINALIZED B | CONSTRUCTION FINALIZED C |

EXHIBITION OPENED D

EXHIBITION MANAGED E

| PROJECT REVIEWED F |
| EXHIBITS RETURNED G |

TEMPLATE DEVELOPED H

NEXT YEAR'S BUDGET APPROVED I

End

Links: ——

Coding: A, B, C, D, E, F, G, H, I

Figure 5

*T*hinking strategically

Up to here we've talked about *what* you do in designing your summary plan. This chapter gives you the detail of *how* you design your summary plan.

THE METHOD – WHERE AND HOW YOU PLAN

Learn to plan on your feet, to move around. Movement frees your body and your mind. We suggest a room large enough to allow you to do this, with sufficient wall space to hold large sheets of flip-chart paper on which you are going to design your plan.

Things you need

Flip-chart paper (worksheets), yellow adhesive self-stick notes, 'Blue-Tac', coloured pens, calendar, plus your sense of humour and listening skills if you are planning with a team.

Why you need them

Blue-tac for sticking the worksheets on the wall. Yellow stickies because you can easily move them around on the worksheets. The alternative to stickies is writing directly onto the worksheets which means erasing or striking out as you change your mind –

adding up to 'confusion'. A selection of coloured pens because you may wish to highlight or colour code different types of data. Flip-chart sheets because they are the worksheets you will head up, stick to the wall, and work on through the planning process.

WORKSHEETS

The core of our planning process is the use of seven worksheets which are in effect a discipline for effective planning. The order is important. The seven worksheets are:

* Worksheet 1 – The visioning process
* Worksheet 2 – The summary plan logic diagram
* Worksheet 3 – Situation analysed (SWOT)
* Worksheet 4 – Resources identified
* Worksheet 5 – Communication plan
* Worksheet 6 – Quality plan
* Worksheet 7 – Project structure

The information generated by these worksheets is collated into what is known as the project document. This becomes the major base reference document for the project. A set of blank worksheets Nos. 1–7 is included at the end of this chapter. You will probably want to have them enlarged to chart size for your planning room wall, particularly if you are working with a project team.

You will use *only* Worksheets 1 and 2 in *designing* the summary plan. The remaining worksheets will be mainly used when you are *developing* your plan. There may be other worksheet headings unique to your project that you will wish to put on charts on the planning wall. Put them all on the wall from the beginning because some detail relating to them will arise from time to time. However, we suggest that you stay as much as possible with the big picture at this stage, encouraging people to stay away from detail.

A TIME FOR STRATEGIC THINKING

In the past, strategic thinking and planning were thought of as something that took place only at the top of an organization.

Nowadays all levels within the organization are expected to deal with strategic planning, that is, each major chunk of work needs to have its overview, its big picture, its summary plan.

Do you see yourself as a strategic thinker or a detailed thinker? The first stage of the planning process, designing the plan, is easier for those who shine in strategic thinking. Those who allow detailed planning to invade this part of their planning process will simply get bogged down. Details are valuable and will be essential at the lower level detailed planning.

As you will see in a moment, details are allowed to intrude; they are not allowed to take over. What you, as planner, are after in the summary stage, is capturing the broad vision, that is, identifying the main chunks of work needed to realize the objective.

People who think in details can have trouble when they try this big picture approach. An accountant we know held his head in dismay: 'Working backwards,' he said, 'I can't do it.' But by the end of a day's planning with a planning facilitator, during which he persisted in the new method and saved many hours, he had changed his attitude completely. Remember the two frogs who fell into a vat of cream? One gave up immediately and drowned, the other persisted in his attempts to escape, thrashing around in the vat until the cream turned to butter and he climbed out (Roger Van Oeck, 'Whack Pack').

Taking care of the detail thinkers

While you are on your feet writing and placing the yellow stickies on the flip-chart sheets, building up your summary diagram with chunks of work, those 'detail thinkers' will also be on the job. Remember, you do not want to take time to discuss details or solve problems. But these details will be essential later, so do not lose them – capture them quickly on the wall charts.

You will not fall into the trap that exists here if you refuse to discuss the details at this time. Let the team know that discussing details will slow you all down, get you off the fast track you are on.

Forgive us for hammering this point. Details are your secondary objective. In the interests of speed, keep your mind on your primary objective which is designing your summary plan. But record the details. As well as having them on your cuff for the next planning stage, you will have kept the 'detail thinkers' happy.

WORKSHEET 1 – THE VISIONING PROCESS

This worksheet is used to document the vision and purpose of the project. During this process the team debates, challenges, suggests, rejects and finally arrives at an acceptable vision and purpose.

You are now ready to begin your summary plan. We envisage you on your feet in front of Worksheet 1. You and your team now focus on reaching agreement on what your vision, that is your overall output, is. The questions that follow are some of the questions that appear on the worksheet itself. Use them to move this process along.

- Where do we want to be in the short term and the long term?
- What is the purpose? Why do we want to be there?

You have completed Worksheet 1 when you have defined the overall output, expressed it in the past tense (for example, 'sales increased') and written it in the box named 'overall output'.

WORKSHEET 2 – THE SUMMARY PLAN LOGIC DIAGRAM

This worksheet is used to document the major chunks of work that are linked in a logical manner.

You wish to produce a summary plan logic diagram on Worksheet 2 on which you will identify the chunks of work to be done to reach the project's objective. Begin by writing your overall output on a yellow sticky and placing it at what will be the end of the summary plan on Worksheet 2.

Now ask the team to consider the impact this overall output will have both inside and outside the company. For example, how would an output, 'sales increased', impact? Inside, will you need more staff, more customer service, larger premises, more training, and so on? Outside, will you have dissatisfied clients and a damaged image?

What is coming out of those questions and answers indicates that increased demand can have a negative impact on the company if those possible eventualities have not been forecast and prepared for. Most important is the way these questions help the team arrive at what has to be done, the chunks of work needed for the project to succeed. Using the 'sales increased' output, chunks of work would obviously include 'staff recruited', 'staff trained', 'premises extended'. As each chunk of work is identified write it on a yellow sticky and place it anywhere on the worksheet.

We suggest at this stage you ask the team to consider the critical success factors by posing the following questions:

● How will we know we have succeeded?
● What will success look like, how will it feel?
● From what and whose perspectives do we need to look at it?

The purpose of these questions is to identify what is critical to the success of this project, and how success will be measured. Chunks of work essential to the factors often emerge at this time. For example, with the output 'sales increased', a critical factor would most likely be 'increased profit' and the chunks of work needed to measure the increase could be 'existing sales analysed', 'sales review procedure developed' and 'sales reviewed'. When you feel the team is satisfied that they have come up with the necessary chunks of work, place the chunks in logical order on Worksheet 2, that is place the chunks in the order in which they have to be done. Do this by simply rearranging the yellow stickies on which you have written the chunks. Use Figures 4 and 5 as a guide.

You will see that Figure 5 shows that the chunk coded H cannot proceed until chunks coded F and G are completed. It is the only kind of linking that concerns you at the moment. Other linking relationships are described in Chapter 4. 'Finish to start relationships' is the term that describes this kind of linking. Now give all the chunks a code, alphabetical or numerical. The coding of each chunk of work at summary level will be particularly useful later in the detailed planning.

SUMMARY

Using our fast-track method to design your summary plan logic diagram, showing coded chunks of work needed to achieve the vision, you:

● Plan on your feet
● Use a series of specially designed worksheets which can be seen by the team, if there is one
● Use questions to establish and challenge the project vision and record it on Worksheet 1
● Avoid becoming involved in discussing detail but capture detail on the appropriate worksheets for future discussion
● Place in haphazard order on Worksheet 2 the yellow stickies on which you have written the chunks of work that will have to be completed
● Place chunks of work in logical order and code the chunks.

In the next chapter you begin the detailed planning of your project.

WORKSHEET 1 – THE VISIONING PROCESS

Start to analyse the situation

Questions:	Answers:

OVERALL OUTPUT

VISION

- Where do we want / need to be in the short and long term?

- What is the purpose?

=

- What will be achieved?

Critical success factors

=

• • • • • •

- How will we know we have succeeded?

- What will success look like, how will it feel?

- From what and whose perspective do we need to look at it?

Page:	of	Draft No:	Dated:	Completed by:

Figure 6

WORKSHEET 2 – THE SUMMARY PLAN LOGIC DIAGRAM

Start

End

Note 'chunks' of work should include:

- Admin type tasks
- Work type tasks
- Monitoring and control type tasks
- Quality tasks

| Page: | of | Draft No: | Dated: | Completed by: |

Use this worksheet to plot 'chunks' of work needing to be completed to meet the vision and deal with impacts

Figure 7

WORKSHEET 3 - SITUATION ANALYSED (SWOT)

	Strengths	Weaknesses	Opportunities	Threats	Links / Effects
1. Overall					
2. Per chunk					
Code					
Code					
Code					
Page: of	Draft No:	Dated:	Completed by:		

Figure 8

WORKSHEET 4 – RESOURCES IDENTIFIED

Chunk description	People skills	Materials	Equipment	Time	Cost
Code					
Code					
Code					

*Note: General admin, project planning and management and general project overheads should be added.

Page:	of	Draft No:	Dated:	Completed by:

Figure 9

46

WORKSHEET 5 – COMMUNICATION PLAN

Description	What	Why	Who to	How	When	By whom	General comment
Overall							
Per chunk							

(use one sheet per chunk for complex chunks)

Page:	of	Draft No:	Dated:	Completed by:

Figure10

WORKSHEET 6 – QUALITY PLAN

Description	Quality requirements	Quality measurement	Responsibility	Comments

Page: ____ of ____   Draft No: ____   Dated: ____   Completed by: ____

Figure 11

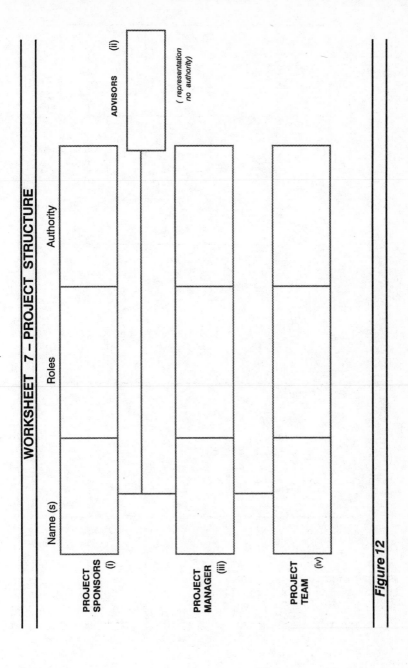

WORKSHEET 7 – PROJECT STRUCTURE

Figure 12

49

PART 3 | *D*EVELOP THE SUMMARY PLAN (DETAILED PLANNING)

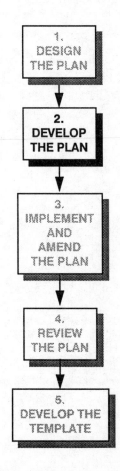

CHAPTER

4

Detailed planning

When you begin developing your plan you are in fact planning in detail the chunks of work you identified in your project summary plan. These become your sub-plans and become part of the planning document.

This chapter has some useful guidelines that will steer you as you begin your detailed planning.

DEVELOPING SUB-PLANS

It is essential that each of the sub-plans is seen by its planner or planners as part of the whole project. Where the person who designed the top level summary plan is not the person doing the detailed planning, it is easy for sub-planners to work in isolation. Ultimately it is the sub-planner's responsibility to make sure they know and understand both the overall big picture of the main project and their place in it.

Links and effects

Knowing and understanding the overall big picture of the main project and their place in it is not enough, however. Wherever you are in the planning process you need to keep yourself informed about what is going on in your organization.

In many organizations considerable effort is wasted because

of the duplication of work. For example, two people in different divisions of an organization were, unknown to each other, both monitoring pollution in their harbour for quite different reasons. To conserve resources you as planners should make it your business to find out if similar work is going on or has been done elsewhere. Does your organization have a database of projects? Do your divisional managers keep a finger on the pulse of the work of other divisions? In some organizations, managers are reluctant to let their thinking and planning stretch beyond the boundaries of their own function. Links of similarity can lead to sharing, which in turn can help put a project on the fast track and yield a more cost-effective return.

Next, effects. Ask yourself about what is going on, both inside the organization and externally, that will affect your project or, similarly, that will be affected by your project. For instance, if your project will put new technology in place it may affect your company premises and staffing, with some skills no longer needed. An example of external effects could be that the schedule of a printer in Hong Kong might affect the publication date of a book published in the United Kingdom. So, having identified possible effects, you put in place a strategy to deal with the possible constraint.

Here is an experience we had. It concerns the effect of someone else's work on one of our own projects. We were writing our first book, *A Practical Guide to Project Management*. Our vision was 'Book used by readers by a certain date'. The summary plan defined the chunks of work as follows: research completed; chapter outlines completed; book proposal submitted; contract signed; chapters written; diagrams completed; **MS edited; cover designed and approved; marketing strategy completed; final MS approved; printing completed; book distributed.**

The publishers were responsible for the detailed planning of the chunks shown in bold print. Thinking ahead, we asked questions of the publisher:

- How long will it take to complete each of the publisher's chunks?
- What are the likely problem areas that will hold up the publisher's part of the process?

That way, in our own detailed planning, thinking strategically at all levels of the project, we were able to set deadlines that allowed for the effects of printing hold-ups.

The result of strategic thinking with regard to links and effects is that plan mechanisms can be put in place.

Vision matching

From the top planner down, planners need to match their respective visions, that is, individual project visions need to match up with divisional and functional visions, and the divisional and functional visions need to match the organizational short- and long-term vision. The effect of not matching up the visions is that the project may be:

- On the wrong track
- Without the support of senior management and therefore likely to be starved of resources.

Some organizations use full-time planners. The planner says 'This is what has to be done', 'This is how long you've got', 'This is what it will cost'. Lack of understanding on the part of the project worker/s can lead to lack of commitment and confusion and may inadvertently sabotage the project.

At all levels of the project, everyone involved in the project should have the big picture, should know where their piece of the picture fits in, should know what it is dependent on, what it links up with, what it will affect.

When you are engaged in detailed planning of a chunk or chunks of work, if you have not been provided with the summary plan (the overview of the whole project), seek out information and make up your own big picture (ask 'Am I understanding this correctly?'). That way, thinking strategically as you begin to develop your part of the plan, you can build factors that ensure a coordinated effort.

Obviously, different chunks of work will have a different number of levels of detail, depending on the complexity of the chunk. The second level of some may be a simple 'to-do' list. Others may require a number of levels of logic diagram.

Working at these lower levels, repeat the planning process outlined in the previous chapters. Develop one chunk of work at a time. In our own experience, using a chunk of work from output 'our books used by readers' we began making a lower level summary plan for the chunk of work identified as 'contract signed' (the vision for this level). Figure 13 shows three levels of summary planning that would have been produced on several copies of Worksheet 2.

Continue to repeat the detailed planning process at the lower levels on your new chunks of work.

How much detail is needed?

The quick answer is, plan to the level at which your project is easily manageable. A rule of thumb is that at detailed working plan level no chunk of work should have a duration of longer than five days.

This question about the level of detail is often asked. In general, the level depends on the project and your own experience.

Here is an account of our experience with a group of scientists. Scientists traditionally are averse to planning. They say there are too many unknowns. In this case, the output of their project was required by a certain time. They attempted to plan, but did not go far enough. At a fairly high level of the planning process, the scientists committed themselves to meeting the client's deadline. Only when it came to planning the resources they would need, using Figure 9 (Worksheet 4 – resources identified chart), did it become obvious that simultaneous testing could not be carried out because of lack of equipment. This lengthened the project duration from three to six months.

That is what we meant by saying the level of detail often depends on your own experience. It also depends on the requirements of your project.

Summary

In approaching the detailed planning of your project you:

- Think in terms of different levels of chunks of work taken from the summary plan
- Establish the vision for the chunk (the sub-plan) you are working on and match that vision with the vision of the project summary plan
- Identify links and effects of this sub-project
- Complete your planning down to the lowest level detail at which your plan can be easily managed.

The next chapter features Worksheet 3 – situation analyzed (SWOT).

PLANNING LEVELS – EXAMPLE

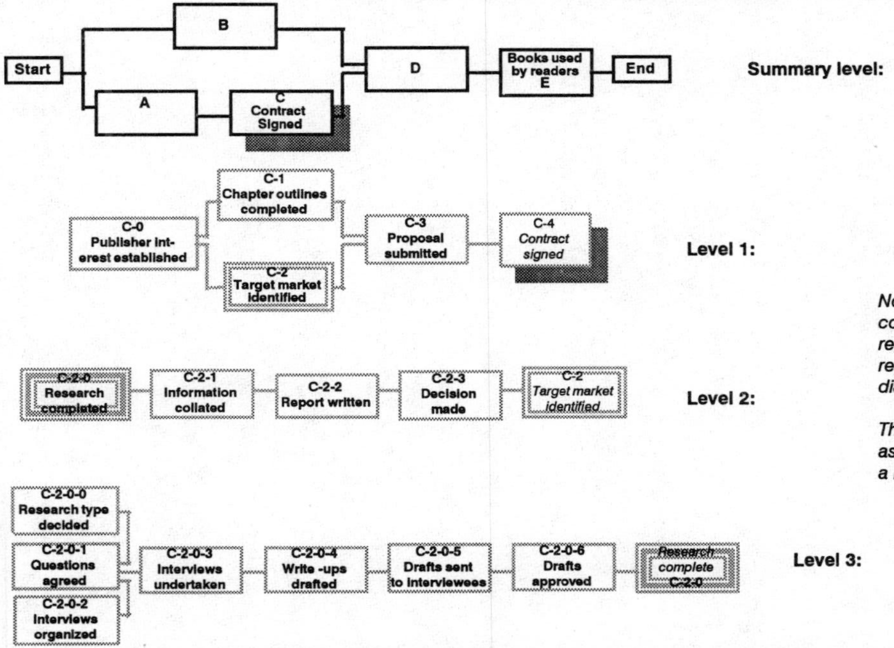

Summary level:

Start

A

B

C Contract Signed

D

Books used by readers E

End

Level 1:

C-0 Publisher Interest established

C-1 Chapter outlines completed

C-2 Target market identified

C-3 Proposal submitted

C-4 Contract signed

Level 2:

C-2-0 Research completed

C-2-1 Information collated

C-2-2 Report written

C-2-3 Decision made

C-2 Target market identified

Level 3:

C-2-0-0 Research type decided

C-2-0-1 Questions agreed

C-2-0-2 Interviews organized

C-2-0-3 Interviews undertaken

C-2-0-4 Write-ups drafted

C-2-0-5 Drafts sent to interviewees

C-2-0-6 Drafts approved

Research complete C-2-0

Note: Some chunks are more complex than others. Some require just lists; others require a number of logic diagrams.

The different levels would normally appear as separate plans with the coding used as a link and identifier.

Figure 13

*T*he SWOT analysis

Worksheet 3, as are all the worksheets, is used at all levels of project planning, that is, in the original summary plan and for all subsequent sub-projects

WORKSHEET 3 – SITUATION ANALYSED (SWOT)

You did your first-cut situation analysis on Worksheet 1 – the visioning process (Figure 6). Begin your detailed planning on Worksheet 3. This worksheet is used to determine strengths, weaknesses, opportunities and threats (SWOT). It is used widely in marketing. It is also used in business planning. Using this worksheet, more often than not you will determine whether there is anything outside as well as inside the organization that will impact on the project, both in the long and short term. Knowing the strengths, weaknesses, opportunities and threats also helps you to develop strategy (how are we going to realize our vision?). As a result of the SWOT analysis, you may find it necessary to add chunks of work to the first cut of your summary plan.

Figure 14 (Worksheet 3 – situation analysed) shows the completed worksheet when SWOT has been applied to the art gallery's summary plan. As with all of the worksheets the SWOT analysis is applied to chunks of work where relevant, i.e. in general terms it would not be relevant for a chunk of work such as 'report approved'.

SITUATION ANALYSED (SWOT) – ART GALLERY EXAMPLE

	Strengths	Weaknesses	Opportunities	Threats	Links / Effects
1. Overall	national popularity commitment national support network	understaffed, funding unknown timeframe short	profit, souvenir sales publicity – image building	other exhibitions lack of sponsorship lack of local demand bad publicity failure to open on time	other exhibitions within gallery shared resources and workspace
2. Per chunk Construction finalized Code c	labour plentiful volunteers, low cost previous experience of similar work	timing unknowns re sponsorship	to loan exhibits and stands wherever possible	lack of space on site timely supply of materials	tradesmen and other exhibitions in house
Code					
Code					

Figure 14

| **Under the microscope**

WORKSHEET 4 – RESOURCES IDENTIFIED

This worksheet is used to identify resources needed for each chunk of work. When you are identifying resource requirements you are estimating, recommending and forecasting what resources are required to achieve each chunk of work within the whole project.

By 'resources' we mean skills, material, equipment, time, money. Remember to include the cost of and time needed for general administration, project planning and management, and general project overheads. As a guide for these, we suggest that you add at least 15 per cent of the total estimate of time and money. For example if the total cost is £100,000 add £15,000.

Estimating resources

Using the art gallery scenario, in Figure 15 (Worksheet 4 – resources identified) we show you what this worksheet looks like when you have done a first cut estimate of resource requirements for each chunk of work.

The first column is headed 'Chunk description'. It lists chunks of work transferred from the summary plan logic diagram. We have developed only one of these: 'Construction finalized'. You will see in the column headed 'Skills' the skills needed to produce that particular chunk. You will also see that it was only a short step then to teaming up skills and people, both internal and external to the gallery. It follows that it is only a short step from knowing the skills needed to matching them up with people.

RESOURCES IDENTIFIED – ART GALLERY EXAMPLE

Chunk description	Skills	Materials	Equipment	Time	Cost
Project set up and approved **Code** [A]				20 days	
Funding and design finalized [B]				60 days	
Construction finalized [C]	Architect, carpenters, builders, printers, coordinators	Construction materials Dust cloths, exhibits	Building related Camera, insurance	20 days	awaiting quotes
Exhibition opened [D]				0 days (milestone)	

*Note: General admin, project planning and management and general project overheads should be added.

Page: of	Draft No:	Dated:	Completed by:

Figure15

At the end of the first cut of resource requirements, copies of the worksheet are made and distributed to the people responsible for each chunk. These people then become responsible for detailed planning and second-cut estimates of materials, equipment, time and cost. On the basis of these second cut estimates, the first cut figures on Worksheet 4 are negotiated and possibly the first cut amended.

The use of historical data concerning previous similar work, plus the experience of the estimator, reduce the risk of miscalculation.

As a lone planner you may have to do the first- and second-cut estimates yourself. First cut is a guesstimate, before any detailed thinking has been done, with an expected margin of error of, say, plus or minus 25 per cent.

Second cut is more informed – you have gone into more detail, asked questions, compared your project with similar work, probably done a feasibility study – margin of error of plus or minus 10 per cent. This can be further improved to plus or minus 5 per cent during implementation stage as you refine and redefine your forecasts.

An estimate of a chunk of project work includes:

- Duration (time it will take from start to finish)
- Skills (level of skill will affect timing and cost)
- Equipment, materials
- Cost
- Contingencies (effect on time and cost)
- Quality requirements (level of quality will affect time and cost)
- Risk (of not meeting, say, cost, time, quality requirements)
- Constraints

Warning. You are failing to get the full picture when you look at each of the above items in isolation. For example:

- Very high standards of quality increase the risk of not completing on time
- Reworking to meet quality standards increases time and cost.

Some planners tend to overlook the very real cost in time and money of administering both planning and implementation. This cost should be included in the estimate.

Another trap planners can fall into concerns the availability of staff. In one case we know of, a person identified as being the one to manage a certain project was already timetabled full-time on other duties. He committed himself to the project. His willingness compounded the difficulty. In fact, of the three months for which he was needed, he was available for the equivalent of only four days. He knew he was busy, of course, but he and the planner failed to work out his true availability. Figure 16 will assist you in assessing how much time you have available.

Scheduling

When you have estimated the durations for each chunk of work (the time column in Worksheet 4), enter the duration for each chunk on your logic diagram on Worksheet 2 (see example in Figure 17).

Using CPM (critical path method), calculate the duration of the whole project and identify critical areas. Critical areas are where chunks of work, if not completed on time, affect the end date of the project.

Identifying the critical path

This involves calculation of what are known as the 'forward pass' and the 'backward pass'. Figure 18 shows how each chunk of work on the logic diagram needs to be marked to allow for calculation of the forward and backward pass. The forward and backward pass calculation determines earliest and latest starts of each chunk of work and allows identification of critical areas (the critical path).

To calculate a forward pass follow steps 1–6 using Figure 19 as a guide.

1. For the first task take the project start date and enter it in the earliest start cell and the latest start cell

2. Now enter the durations for each task in each duration cell

3. Add the duration for Task A to the earliest start and enter the resultant date in the earliest finish cell

REAL TIME AVAILABLE

Based on:

7.5 hours per day, 5 days per week, 52 weeks per year

Less:

10 days statutory holidays, 20 days annual leave, 5 days sick

= 45 working weeks = 1687.5 hours per year

Less:

unproductive meetings, dealing with phone calls, travel to and from appointments, sorting out conflict, looking for things, rework, etc. Productivity rate reduced by 40%

= **1012 . 5 hours**

Cost per hour based on annual salary of £16,000 with an overhead factor of 2: **£31.60**

Figure 16

SUMMARY PLAN – EXAMPLE SCHEDULE

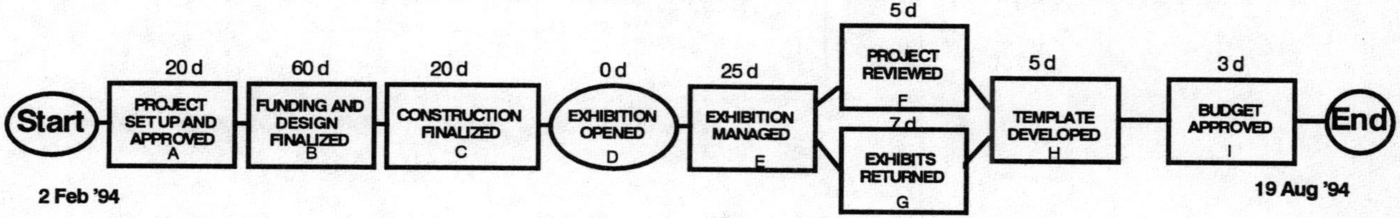

Based on one person full-time per parcel of work and on working days only.

Figure 17

SCHEDULING – TASK BOX

ES = earliest start

EF = earliest finish

ES	Duration	EF
CODE	Task name	
LS	Slack	LF

LS = latest start

LF = latest finish

Figure 18

4. Enter the earliest finish date from the previous task in the earliest start cell of the following task. Where there are several previous tasks, as in Task E, take the latest date.

5. Repeat the calculation for each successive task

6. Enter the earliest finish date for the last task in the latest finish cell of this task.

To calculate a backward pass follow steps 1–3 using Figure 20 as a guide.

1. Start at the last task (Task E) and subtract the duration from the latest finish date of that task. Enter the result in the latest start cell of that task.

2. Enter the latest start date from last task (Task E) in the latest finish date of the previous task or tasks (Tasks C and D).

3. Repeat steps 1 and 2 for each task, working backwards to Task A.

Calculate slack time by deducting the earliest start time from the latest start time or by deducting the earliest finish time from the latest finish time. The critical path is identified where slack time is '0'.

Summary

Information from Worksheet 4 – resources identified is used to:

- Estimate resources
- Schedule resources on Worksheet 2
- Disseminate information about resources to specific project workers who are required to validate the first-cut estimate
- Calculate the duration of the project and identify the critical path.

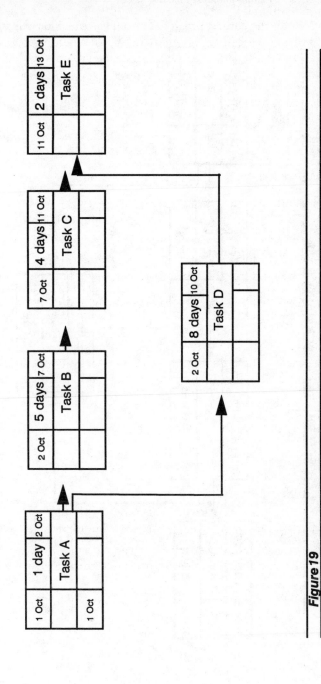

Figure 19

69

SCHEDULING – BACKWARD PASS

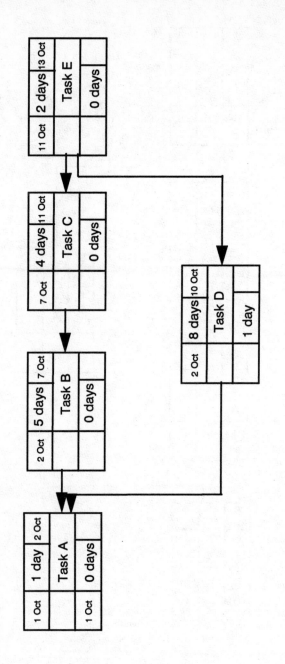

Figure 20

*P*utting everyone in the picture

WORKSHEET 5 – COMMUNICATION PLAN

A communication plan is part of the project plan. Worksheet 5 is used to set out all facets of communication relating to the project. Questions the team may discuss during this process are:

- What needs to be communicated?
- How should it be communicated (presentation, radio, memo, etc.)?
- When should it be communicated?
- Who should be informed?
- How do we get feedback to ensure the message is received and understood?
- Who is/are responsible for sending the message and collating and acting on feedback?

We emphasize that communication is a two-way procedure. We send messages. We receive messages. It sounds so simple. Yet between the sending and receiving often lies a morass of misunderstanding. Put time and care into your communication plan.

When a lorry broke down at the side of the road a passing motorist stopped to help. He had this load of penguins to take to the zoo, the lorry driver said. The motorist offered to take them and the grateful lorry driver thanked him and gave him some money for expenses. Later, when he reached the city, the lorry driver saw the helpful motorist on the street with the ten penguins trailing along behind him. 'Hey,' he said to the motorist, 'You said you would take the penguins to the zoo.' The motorist looked surprised. 'I took them to the zoo,' he said. 'There was some money left and now we're going to the movies.'

It is the responsibility of the person sending or giving the message to check that they have transferred their meaning. A communication plan is a critical component of the planning process and should have a feedback mechanism built into it. How else do you know your message has been received and understood? Communication breaks down when one of these five 'C's' is missing:

- Complete
- Correct
- Clear
- Courteous
- Concise.

The data you are generating on your communication worksheet may become part of each chunk of work, or, if the communication requirements are major, you may have decided to set communication out as a path within the whole summary plan as shown in Figure 21.

We are now going to leave the art gallery example and invite you to read 'Operation Krypton'. Other factors may interest you in the case, but we particularly ask you to concentrate on the communication aspects.

CASE 2 – OPERATION KRYPTON

Operation Krypton could be said to have been based on hope. And for those of the 20,000 long-term unemployed 18–25-year-old registered job seekers who took up the challenge of six weeks in the armed forces, it provided hope – in the form of life skills. After six weeks they left the army, navy or air force with heightened awareness of their own potential and worth. They left with a knowledge of the value of discipline and self-discipline. For the first time some of them learned about team work. They developed responsibility, initiative and skills for day-to-day activities.

So the question must be asked: with so much on offer by the New Zealand Defence Force in conjunction with New Zealand

Employment Services Ltd, with so much going for Operation Krypton, why was it so nearly a disaster in its implementation?

The scheme was approved by the government in late March and opened for applications on 26 April. Since the Defence Force was working in conjunction with the Employment Office, there would be no need to advertise.

The response was abysmal. With only a week to the start of training, only 20 eligible to join had signed up. This provoked the comment from a senior Defence Force staff member that the organizers were forced to assume that the target groups would not accept the challenge of real adventure and instead preferred to stick to the safety of their video games.

Yes, but... some members of the target group complained that the application forms were not available, that it was hard to get information about the course (whom did you ring?), that sort of thing. The mother of one interested young person rang the Employment Office. Yes, they said, they knew about Operation Krypton but had no information about it. The free toll number they provided responded with a recorded message. By the date of return of the person leaving the message, the first course would have started.

Back to the Employment Office. They had another number, this time for one of the service bases, which involved a toll call. The public relations person at that number was out. The caller requested to be put through to anyone who might be able to help – striking gold: an enthusiastic person familiar with details of the scheme. The toll call took just under half an hour.

Would a young unemployed person short of self-confidence and money have got past the first hurdle?

Financial factors kept some people away. Who, if anyone, counselled the young unemployed that while the Training Benefit was less than the Unemployment Benefit by £50 a week, the return was better: three good meals a day, access to training and advice from some eighteen different agencies ranging from the Red Cross to banks, as well as the expertise of the armed forces in adventure training and outdoor activities? For some there was also the question of rent that had to be paid to retain rooms and flats to come back to. Were supplementary benefits available? No-one seemed to know.

The senior head office organizer at Defence was most cooperative and forthcoming in discussing what went wrong. Of course, the important thing was that it was put right, but unfortunately at a cost, such as the poor press Krypton got at the time.

It appears that the major flaw was in the planning process. For example, in matters military the Defence Force operates on management-by-project. Operation Krypton, on the other hand,

COMMUNICATION PATH ON LOGIC DIAGRAM – EXAMPLE

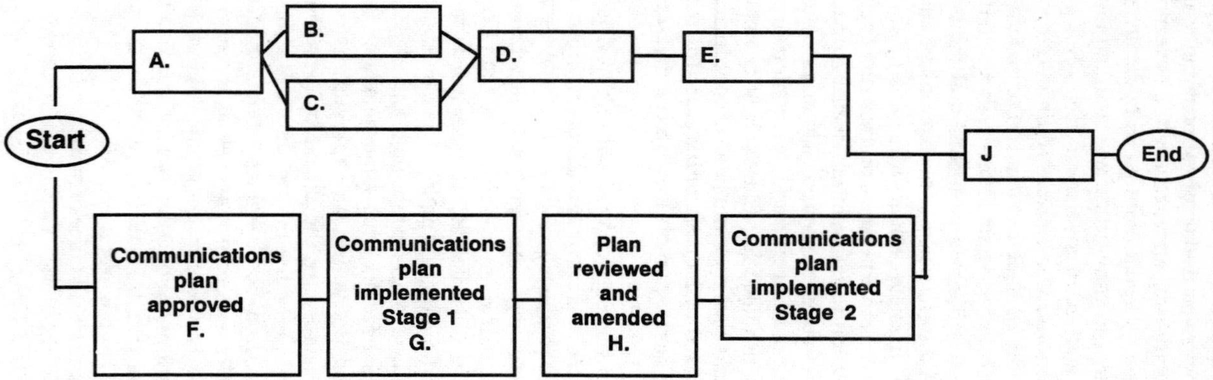

Figure 21

appeared to be run on management-by-objective lines. That is to say, there was no use of formal planning tools such as the logic diagram and the Gantt chart.

There was a team, of course, made up of a representative each from all involved organizations – armed forces, health, public relations and employment services – but everyone on it was drawn from head office staffs. No representatives of the unemployed were involved in the planning process; there was no-one there to ask, 'But what about me?'

At the top there were the cabinet ministers for whom the scheme had top priority. At strategic planning level, operations personnel from the three forces had responsibility for setting objectives and 'do-by' dates, and for advising the facilitators who would be running the training. From their point of view a contingency plan should have been essential. In fact, military matters arose that pushed Operation Krypton off the top priority list for operations. Should not personnel have been running the show?

Then there was the question of coordination. Because all the forces were putting courses together for the first time for the young unemployed, you could say they were all engaged in inventing the wheel. Yet time was critical and they all had the same goals. A joint effort, with everyone focused on the same outcome, would have saved time, money and effort without diminishing flexibility.

Much of what went wrong with this project could have been identified early in the planning if the right people had been involved (not necessarily operations) and their efforts had been better coordinated.

When and if something similar to Operation Krypton is planned, a project management approach would be advisable. Essential to the success of the scheme are:

● The make-up of the team
● Success criteria
● Communication strategy (including a feedback strategy)
● Marketing strategy.

For a successful outcome, within the communication strategy, involve from an early planning stage those most affected – the unemployed – with whom clear two-way communication would be essential.

In Krypton, a communication plan would have been worth its weight in gold. That is why we chose Krypton to demonstrate Worksheet 5 (Figure 22). It shows how one chunk of work from the logic diagram could appear on the worksheet.

COMMUNICATION PLAN – EXAMPLE, KRYPTON PROJECT

Description	What	Why	Who to	How	When	By whom	General comment
Overall							
Marketing Info. and forms tested B	Content of material tested	to ensure: • understanding • accuracy • relevance • completeness • effect	representatives of each interested or affected party including the unemployed	• send samples out for comment • hold meetings • have people complete forms	before first media release	Public relations support staff	

Page 1 of 6 | Draft No: 1 | Dated: 2/2/94 | Completed by: C Burton

(use one sheet per chunk for complex chunks)

Figure 22

77

CHAPTER 8 | Quality standards

WORKSHEET 6 – QUALITY PLAN

This worksheet is used to define the quality standards required of both the product and the service surrounding it, and to establish procedures to ensure that the quality is there. Take the example of a report as the product. The quality criteria of the report may be specified within the five 'C's' of communication (conciseness, courtesy of tone, correctness, clarity of meaning and completeness); for the service the criteria may measure the effectiveness of the distribution and the obtaining of timely feedback and action arising from the feedback.

In our planning, we identify and allow for the resources and procedures by which we will control quality. We ask questions: 'How will quality be achieved?' 'How do we know if we have reached the required standard?' We answer them: 'By setting criteria', 'By using measurable standards'. We also ask, 'Does the organization have the ability to meet the standards?'

Sometimes quality standards need to be looked at from different perspectives. For example, a computer program designer may set quality criteria for a client. The user, however, may have their own perception of quality. Which adds up to dissatisfied client. Sometimes as part of your planning it is necessary to build in precautionary measures to reduce that risk.

In the next case study you will see the approach that furniture designer/manufacturer, John Ahearn, takes to ensure that clients get what they need as well as what they want, and that John himself gets paid.

CASE 3 – THE ONE-MAN BAND

John, who designs and manufactures office, restaurant and bar furniture, uses project planning in managing the many facets of his business. He works on many levels and relies heavily on his network of highly skilled sub-contractors which includes steel fabricators, wood workers, upholsterers and powder coaters. His competition in this highly competitive business includes small manufacturers like himself, plus large companies, geared to total in-house production, who are also producing restaurant, bar and office furniture. John has the edge over the big companies who have higher overheads and productivity restricted to the capacity of their in-house resources. John's overheads are low and he has unlimited external resources.

John has also achieved a competitive advantage by his speed of service and the quality control which he has built into his planning.

The speed of service comes from the preferential treatment he gets from his network of sub-contractors who will often stop a current job to do a rush job for him. He has gained credibility with them. He is dependable. He consistently pays his bills on time.

Regarding quality control, John's maxim is: you don't make a living if you get paid once and do the job twice, so he builds quality into the whole manufacturing process, and goes one step further, personally delivering the furniture components and, with his team, assembling it on the client's site. Add to this that a couple of days later he visits the client to see that everything is satisfactory, and, if it is not, puts it right. Thus he ensures a sound project wind-up, encourages prompt payment and enhances his own manufacturing image. Satisfied clients mean word-of-mouth advertising. Advertising means increased business. John has faced this question and part of his long-term planning is determining how to maintain quality and meet increased demand.

In John's business, the high risk is in the area of design, of getting it right for the client. Always, of course, he wants to give the client a quality job, but sometimes clients ask for a design which, manufactured, would not be what they really want. Sometimes they turn a deaf ear to his advice. So John ensures they are getting what they need by following a process that begins with showing them a mock-up model. If they approve that then he goes ahead and puts a prototype on site that is as close to the finished product as possible. The client sees the design in the environment for which it is intended.

In one case where John was responsible for the manufacture of fifty bar stools, the bar owner engaged an architect to do the design – John became a third party. The architect was John's client. John thought the design was a bit off. He said so. His client disagreed. As John is not in the business of losing clients, he went ahead, produced the mock-up and the prototype which he put on site. As he expected, amendments were necessary.

Furthermore, in that situation, as project manager, John was prepared to accept responsibility for the whole project, including the original faulty design.

In this case study, in his planning process, John Ahearn built in chunks of works that controlled quality at each stage of design and manufacture, including delivery, installation and follow-up. That is standard practice for John. That way, he has his finger on the pulse and can correct errors as they arise, thus reducing the risk of clients seeing him as doing a poor job for them. These quality mechanisms cost John time and money. He has proved they are worth it.

International Quality Requirements – ISO9000

More and more organizations are moving towards the use of internationally recognized standards of quality control. One of these sets of standards, the ISO9000 (International Standards Organization) is widely accepted. Accreditation by this organization means that you undertake to comply consistently with the standard of quality you have written. Also, that you will have an on-going internal audit as well as agreeing to being randomly audited by the ISO. Synergy International Limited, of which co-author Celia Burton is a director, has just completed their accreditation process. Treating the accreditation process as a planned and controlled project shortened the usual time considerably. The whole staff had a focus on specific quality-related roles. A sub-chunk of work included developing a communication plan because accreditation is a marketable product.

In Figure 23 we use a chunk of work from each of Cases 2 and 3 to demonstrate the use of the quality plan.

QUALITY PLAN – EXAMPLE

Description	Quality requirements	Quality measurement	Responsibility	Comments
Bar furniture completed	Customer satisfied in the short and long term	Sign off during design and prototyping, after delivery and after 6 months	Designer manufacturer	
Brochures produced	Easily understood Generates interest Accuracy of information	Tested by users Approved by sponsors and users	Public relations	

Page: of   Draft No: Dated: Completed by:

Figure 23

*S*uccessful teamwork

WORKSHEET 7 – PROJECT STRUCTURE

This worksheet is used as a guide to help you identify the official set-up of people within the project. It delineates responsibilities and authority. Its purpose is to clarify roles, to build a unified team and to reflect the needs of the project. By the latter, we mean you structure your project in such a way as to avoid or minimize the possibility of problems that were identified during your detailed planning. The structure of the project evolves from all the information generated by the planning process.

Here are two examples of how and why project structures were set up.

Example 1

A $40 million project involved a regional and local authority merging to implement a district scheme. During the planning process planners identified the possibility of conflict between the two authorities, a 'them' and 'us' situation, with pride and power at stake, therefore overt and covert objectives, when what was necessary was a team approach. Also the public were likely to oppose the particular option the authorities had chosen. With so many involved, decision making loomed as a problem, as did quality control. There were other 'people' problems: work overload combined with a critical time schedule.

In their project structure, the planners tackled the above

problems by setting up, for the duration of the project, a separate company, in a separate location, in which everyone was seen to play a role that was removed from their regional or local position.

You can see that leaving the skilled people needed for the project in their regular habitats would have been fatal. Working in overload gear as they were, their other work would have had preference. They coped in part by working regular hours on the project. We will come back to this example shortly.

Example 2

Consider corporate lawyers working on international sales and mergers. Because mergers are usually time-critical and involve multiple clients, lawyers can structure these projects so that the perception is that everyone involved is playing a part. They may do this because the solicitors do not want the 'them' and 'us' attitude mentioned in Example 1 to prevail during negotiations. It is the structure that they set up during the merger that enables the clients as well as the lawyers to feel part of the team. In a sense it means everyone sees themselves as being part of the big picture and committed to it. They are more interested in seeing the merger proceed than in apportioning blame when problems arise. Knowing the critical areas, knowing the effects of delayed responses, is the spur that keeps the project rolling.

The structure in Example 1 (Worksheet 7) could look like Figure 24.

In Example 1 (Figure 24) the planning consultants recommended that at the top decision-making level (box [i] in the diagram), there should be not more than four people, that a senior technical staff member should be included to represent each of the two authorities, a third person to chair the group (perhaps the mayor), with a fourth being possibly a financial adviser. Next step down would be an advisory group representing interested groups, that is people affected by the project (box [ii]). These people would have no authority. Their position on the diagram illustrates that they communicate not only with the project manager (box [iii]), who may be biased, but with the senior group at the top. The project team (box [iv]) may be made up of leaders responsible for specific chunks of work.

PROJECT STUCTURE – EXAMPLE 1

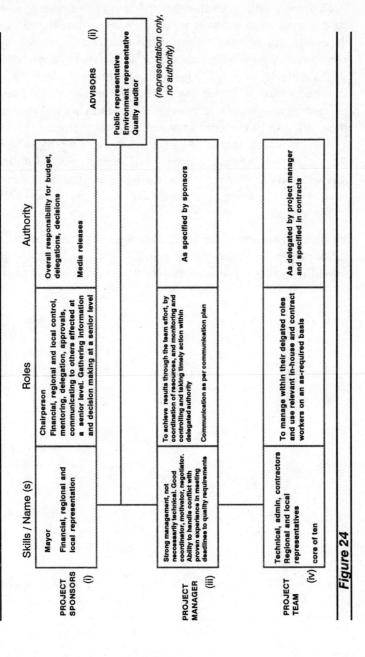

	Skills / Name (s)	Roles	Authority
PROJECT SPONSORS (i)	**Mayor** Financial, regional and local representation	**Chairperson** Financial, regional and local control, mentoring, delegation, approvals, communicating to others affected at a senior level. Gathering information and decision making at a senior level	Overall responsibility for budget, delegations, decisions Media releases
			ADVISORS (ii) Public representative Environment representative Quality auditor *(representation only, no authority)*
PROJECT MANAGER (iii)	Strong management, not neccessarily technical. Good coordinator, motivator, negotiator. Ability to handle conflict with proven experience in meeting deadlines to quality requirements	To achieve results through the team effort, by coordination of resources, and monitoring and controlling and taking timely action within delegated authority Communication as per communication plan	As specified by sponsors
PROJECT TEAM (iv)	Technical, admin, contractors Regional and local representatives core of ten	To manage within their delgated roles and use relevant in-house and contract workers on an as-required basis	As delegated by project manager and specified in contracts

Figure 24

85

Obviously, although the concept of project structure should be common to all projects, all projects are different and Figure 24 would not be suitable for all. In Example 2, we have seen corporate lawyers pulling their hair as due dates arrive without vital replies from clients. Their project structure would include the information set out in box [i], that is, the names of the representatives of clients and lawyers, their roles within that team (box [ii]), and the extent of the authority of each one (box [iii]). The team would share the responsibility of keeping to guidelines that met the requirements and expectations of both the lawyers and the clients. The clients would feel part of the project from the beginning and would be much more likely to be committed to it.

You are almost across the line. Some project planners would say, '... 99 percent of the way – for ever!!' Near enough is not good enough, however. The next chapter deals with the 1 per cent.

*T*he last brush strokes

THE FINAL 1 PER CENT

Where are you now? You have designed and developed your plan almost to completion; you have a summary plan logic diagram, plus all the information generated on the worksheets. The plan essentials listed in this chapter fall outside the scope of the summary plan and the worksheets, but without these essentials that remaining 1 per cent short of completion we mentioned may remain just that. Their importance justifies giving them a chapter of their own.

From the information you have generated, you will have identified problems and constraints and critical success factors such as, short term, time, and, long term, image.

One common constraint on any project is the priority status the project holds (actual versus perceived). As outlined below, the status allocated to your project coupled with the critical success factors will determine project pace and achievement.

Setting priorities

The perception of priority status differs across the organization. Ideally, priorities should be set at the top and fed downwards. Often they are not. When they are not, then the planner must make a point of establishing the priority and feeding it upwards for approval.

Priority status has a direct impact on project risk. Using the information generated on your worksheets during the planning process, you will decide whether you are engaged in a high-risk project, that is, a project that is in danger of succumbing to any or all of the following risk factors:

- Not achieving goals
- Not being completed on time
- Not getting approvals
- Not going smoothly.

So in light of the risk, you need to set project priorities. A low priority project has a higher chance of failure or non-completion because appropriate resources may not be assigned or may be taken away during implementation in favour of higher priority work. This removal of resources may affect timing, costing, quality and even morale. High priority projects, which usually have the backing of senior management, are more likely to have first call on resources.

Therefore, think carefully at this stage of how much time and effort you are going to commit to the low priority projects. Let us say you initiate a new project. Look at it in relation to all of the work you and your team are presently committed to. Where does this new project fit in? What priority does it or should it have? If necessary negotiate new priorities for existing projects, keeping in mind that priorities within an organization are often in conflict. At organizational, divisional and individual levels, planners vie for a share of the resources. As part of its management-by-project, an organization needs an agreed procedure for when priorities change whereby all concerned parties are committed to sharing the problem of shared resources and solving the problem together.

Another question is what authority you personally have as a project planner. Authority is power. Your power should reflect the priority level of your project. If you have not got the relative power and are not likely to get it, try to enlist the support of a mentor who has the power.

Failing to set priorities can land you in what is known as an 'activity trap'. In an activity trap, the planner commits to too much. Sets unrealistic goals. One young planner said to us recently, 'I've just got to stop. I've a wife and young child. I've got to keep fit, yet last night I missed my touch rugby game. I've been here in the office all weekend.' One unfortunate result of this kind of willy-nilly approach is that some projects simply fall by the wayside. What a lot of wasted effort!

Remember, sometimes you cannot do everything in the time available.

As well as in preparing your planning document, during implementation you will need to constantly review priorities as work progresses and the situation changes. Details of changed priorities should then be recorded in your project document.

So, in general, prioritize, channel your energies effectively and take the weekend off! As we said, despite the importance of setting project priorities in line with a company's mission statement, top management often fail to set any priorities and as a result, plans may be designed and developed, but never implemented. Or they may fall over during implementation. The following case study demonstrates this very clearly.

CASE 4 – THE SCIENTISTS DISCOVER RESOURCE SCHEDULING

In this science-based research company, the work consists of both short-term and long-term contracts. The resource constraints are mainly funding and people, with the skills needed often having to be imported. On the job, pressure arises from the urgency attaching to short-term projects.

Long-term work, increasingly seen as non-critical, tends to be pushed aside. Since much of the funding depends on the ongoing research of the long-term projects, it is vital these projects should not be neglected. On the other hand, in practice, resources are constantly diverted to meeting the requirements of the short-term demands.

Long-term contracts cannot be met or are short changed. Everyone is in reactive mode. No priorities are being set. No mechanisms exist to identify and deal with overload. The company takes advice. A project team of four people is formed. Their brief: to develop a prototype resource management system. They begin by preparing a twelve-month programme of contracts, both short- and long-term. Then they categorize all the different types of work to be done in the unit and develop templates for each type (See Chapter 13).

Appropriate workers are asked to customize the templates, assign the resources needed against each job and estimate how many work hours per resource are needed. They also have to include in their planning additional short-term jobs, as yet unknown.

The project team then sets up an overheads matrix classifying them by resource (how many hours per resource per week on each type of overhead activity).

The team collate this information and display it on one huge schedule which shows the total resource hours assigned per resource for the duration of the schedule.

When it is discovered that more than 25 per cent of the work hours are in conflict, the 30 people involved in the whole exercise put on their thinking caps. What parts of jobs can be delegated (unskilled jobs taken away from skilled workers)? What extra skilled staff need to be recruited?

The team need a base from which to begin solving these problems. They decide that what is required are criteria by which to set priorities. They also build into their plan a mechanism by which priorities, once established, can be updated as the need arises.

Where priorities are not set at organizational level, the planner must take control, and ask questions:

- What are the priorities of the earlier planned projects?
- Where does the new project fit in?
- Will extra resources be needed?

The planner should then set priorities and feed them back to management stating that these are the priorities as the planner sees them and if they are not correct to please discuss.

Setting up monitoring and control procedures

The development of monitoring and control procedures is part of developing the plan. The act of monitoring and controlling a project is part of managing the project during implementation. Before we get to implementation we need to have identified what has to be monitored and controlled. It is the setting up of procedures we are covering here. First, however, let us define the term 'monitoring and control'.

- Monitoring is where the actual progress on a project is plotted against estimates that are called baselines, and where likely outcomes are forecast.
- Control is where appropriate timely action is taken to achieve appropriate results.

Standard guidelines and procedures within your organization may need to be adapted to suit the specific needs of individual projects because high risk areas and unknowns vary from project to project.

Our understanding of monitoring and control will be enhanced if we know why it is necessary. Figure 25(a) sets out the purpose and control cycle.

You will find Figures 25(b), (c) and (d) useful when you are setting up your monitoring and control procedures.

MONITORING AND CONTROL – PURPOSE

To:

• Provide a basis for management decisions

• Aim at discovering any unplanned departure from the planned course, so that adjustments can be made in time to be effective

• Assess effects of planned change, review feasibility, identify options.

The control cycle:

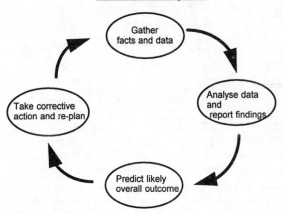

Ref: A guide to process and procedures – International Labour Office Geneva

---

Figure 25(a)

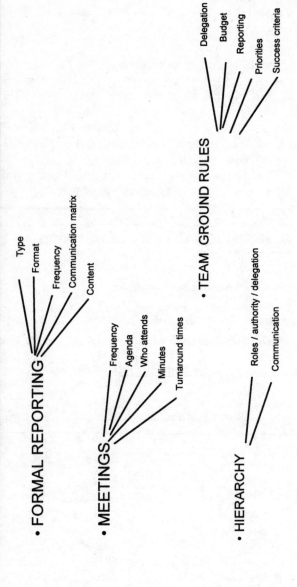

MONITORING AND CONTROL – SET-UP PROCEDURES

- FORMAL REPORTING
  - Type
  - Format
  - Frequency
  - Communication matrix
  - Content

- MEETINGS
  - Frequency
  - Agenda
  - Who attends
  - Minutes
  - Turnaround times

- TEAM GROUND RULES
  - Delegation
  - Budget
  - Reporting
  - Priorities
  - Success criteria

- HIERARCHY
  - Roles / authority / delegation
  - Communication

- Documentation – Files

Figure 25(b)

- Enter estimates into system

- Collect timesheet data

- Enter actual resource time in system

- Forecast work to complete and enter in system

- Identify any actions

- Take action

SYSTEMS AND PROCEDURES ARE WORTHLESS IF NOT
TRANSFERRED
TO ACTION

Figure 25(c)

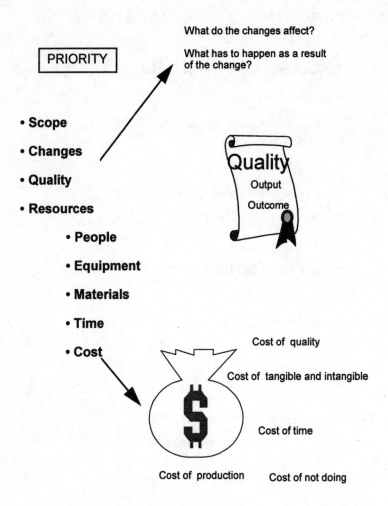

PRIORITY

What do the changes affect?

What has to happen as a result of the change?

- **Scope**
- **Changes**
- **Quality**
- **Resources**
    - **People**
    - **Equipment**
    - **Materials**
    - **Time**
    - **Cost**

Quality
Output
Outcome

Cost of quality

Cost of tangible and intangible

Cost of time

Cost of production   Cost of not doing

Figure 25(d)

Completing the planning document

During the first two planning phases, designing and developing the plan, you will be compiling a working document. This forms a contract for implementing the project plans. The planning document includes:

- Background and purpose
- Statement of objective
- Scope of work and any exclusions
- Project output and sub-outputs
- Critical success factors
- Links and effects
- Predicted problems (defined by SWOT) and strategies to overcome
- Constraints
- High-risk areas
- Priorities
- Resource requirements
- Feasibility and alternative strategies
- Structure
- Roles and authority levels
- Timeframes and costs
- Monitoring and control procedures
- Appendices (supporting plans such as logic diagram, critical path and the Gantt chart).

The end result is a concise working brief that is signed off before implementation. Some planning documents may have gone through a number of approval stages before reaching final sign-off. It is a text-based document, supported by graphic plans, which continues to be used as a base document during implementation of the plan, at which time it is reviewed and updated as necessary. On reflection, perhaps the '99 per cent forever' planners are right!

Summary

In setting priorities you:

- Assess the project's priority status
- Determine the project's risk factors
- Focus your efforts on high-priority projects
- Ensure there is a procedure for negotiating priority changes, particularly where your organization's resources are shared
- Establish that you or a mentor have the authority/power commensurate with your project
- Review existing priorities as work progresses and the situation changes
- Record in your project document priority changes and any necessary ensuing action
- Submit your own priority assessment upwards when top management have failed to assign a priority.

In setting up monitoring and control procedures you:

- Identify what has to be monitored and controlled during implementation of the project
- Define the procedures and tools that will be used to monitor and control the project
- Set up the mechanisms by which information about actuals versus estimates (the baseline) can be collected to enable timely action.

In completing the planning document you:

- Bring together text and diagrams resulting from the planning process.

The next chapter provides guidelines on how to prepare your project document for management and the team. Your purpose is to inform and persuade.

CHAPTER	*T*he work
11	of art

PRESENTING YOUR PROJECT DOCUMENT

You have done it by the book. Designed your plan. Developed it. Had it approved and signed off as you went. Most probably you have celebrated milestones. In this chapter we ask you to consider a) the document itself, and b) how to present it orally.

Written form

HOW DOES IT LOOK, YOUR COMPLETED PROJECT DOCUMENT?
After all the hard work, what do you have to show for it? Well, what you have is something tangible, something you can look at, read, pass around, discuss. Ideally, it is something you are proud of – the project document.

One of the functions of your project document is to help you sell your ideas. For instance you may be presenting a case for resources and a preferred *modus operandi*. The least you want is to have somebody read the document, and the ultimate is to have your plan accepted. To this end, the document should be clear, concise, factual, correct and complete. It should be pleasing to the eye. Its information should be capable of being quickly absorbed and understood, therefore format is important.

If you have just completed a plan, pause now and take another look at this document and ask yourself whether your pride in it is justified or whether there is anything you need to amend to improve its attractiveness to readers.

Have you ever picked up a book, an article, a report, had a quick look, then, involuntarily, put it down? You will keep it for later you probably think, when you have more time. Why is that? What put you off? Most likely the print was too dense, the paragraphs were too long, there were hardly any white spaces and no headings to break up the content. Probably the diagrams were too small and the words on them too hard to read without a magnifying glass. Unless it was absolutely essential that you read the item you most probably never went back to it.

So look around you when you are drafting your project document. Pick the eyes out of documents you like, the ones prepared by other people, and adapt their format, style, layout to suit yourself. What pleased you as a reader will most likely please others. And, as we said earlier, the least you want for your project plan is that it should be read.

Therefore, keep the reader in mind. Present an attractive document. One consultancy we know of is inundated with curricula vitae from aspiring consultants. Going through these c.v.'s management does not muck about. Very quickly there are two piles, the no-goes on the left, on the right, the look-at-again. The no-go pile is full of c.v.'s that at first glance are too hard to read – their owners are obviously not adept at presenting written work, a prerequisite in that consultancy.

You entice readers when you:

- Consider who your readers are, their time commitment (have they got all day to read your document?), their style (vocabulary, etc.), their major interest (financial, operational, etc.)
- Have a clear, uncluttered title page and contents page
- State the purpose of your document, who developed it and when, and who/what will be affected by the project
- Have a summary page
- Have clear headings
- Get to the point quickly – support brief text with appendices
- Avoid jargon, and instead use lively language that instantly captures the reader's attention
- Use a layout that flows and allows readers to find things quickly – include an index and glossary.

Spoken form

At the same time as you distribute the project document, set up a time and place when you will discuss its salient points and answer questions. Tell management that 10 or 15 minutes is all you need. You can probably do it in that time. You may need longer to discuss the document with your project team.

The key to the success of your oral presentation is amazingly simple. It can be summed up in one word: preparation. Preparation helps to remove anxiety about the actual delivery. Free from worry you are more likely to speak confidently and fluently. The next two sections of this chapter deal with those topics: preparation and delivery.

PREPARING THE ORAL PRESENTATION

1. Decide your purpose in speaking. You could have simply distributed your planning document. However, you have decided to back the document up with a spoken presentation. Why is that? The answer to that question will become the purpose of your presentation. The importance of identifying the purpose lies in your then knowing how to target your talk. Once you are clear about the purpose for which you are speaking, you are able to use what is called the correct 'register' or 'voice' – that is, be persuasive, if that is your purpose, or informative, or perhaps encouraging (you want the listeners to ask questions and offer their perspective on the project planning document). So, be clear in your mind about why you are going to the trouble to give an oral presentation. Also:

2. Assess the knowledge of your audience. A useful technique is to get to know the words they use in talking to you, and use those words back to them where relevant in your presentation.

3. Keep their special interest in mind, particularly the degree to which the project will affect them.

4. Identify the visual aids you are going to use. Overhead projector? Flip chart? Whiteboard? The document itself? Whatever you use, practise. Become adept.

5. You may decide to use the document itself instead of notes,

or you may prepare brief notes. In either case, prepare a strong, clear opening and ending.

THE OPENING

- State your topic clearly (you are going to talk about the project document). To stimulate their interest tell the listeners right away, in the fewest words possible, the vision and purpose of the project (if the vision and purpose take more than a total of two sentences, you could consider being more succinct).
- Next, set out the framework of the body of your talk – the headings taken from the planning document that you want to talk about or discuss. It's called 'telling the audience what you're going to tell them'. Your headings might be:

> THE BIG PICTURE
> THE TIMEFRAME
> RESOURCE REQUIREMENTS
> ISSUES AND PROBLEMS/OPPORTUNITIES FROM
> THE PLANNERS' PERSPECTIVE

Have more than four major headings and you are almost certain to lose your audience!

- Lastly, decide when you want the audience to ask questions or to give their perspective on the project, and include a clear direction at the end of your opening.

THE BODY

- Announce each heading as you come to it.
- Move smoothly, using transitional phrases, from one main heading to the next.

THE CLOSING

Tell them what you have told them. Repeat the headings of the body of your talk – the same framework that you set out in your opening. Then, immediately, invite the questions or discussion you told the audience you were keeping to the end.

DELIVERING THE ORAL PRESENTATION

Whether you are speaking to small or large groups, the degree of stress these occasions will cause you will relate to the amount of control you have in this area of oral presentation. The better prepared you are, even to practising your opening words aloud, the more control you will have and the less nervous you will be.

The two main things you have to remember in speaking to groups large or small (you may think they are so obvious as not to merit mention) are that you have to be heard and you have to be understood. With the kindest of intentions ask yourself the question: if it is so obvious, how come so many speakers fail in this regard? Often, even, one to one!

Keeping this need for audibility and intelligibility in mind, and confident that the framework you are using will keep you and the listeners on track, it is safe to say that speaking to a group is really only extended conversation. So be yourself, be audience-oriented. Look at people when you are talking to them. Use the word 'you' often to show that you are thinking of your audience, of how the project may affect them, impinge on them, even alter their work pattern. Get the listeners on your side as much as possible.

You probably do not enjoy listening to monotonous speakers, so make sure you yourself vary your own tone, pace and pitch and inject some vigour into your voice when you are presenting your project document.

One way in which you can make a good impression is to begin strongly and end strongly. It is rather easy for a speaker's voice to trail off at the end of a presentation, and even at the end of sentences.

Question time can be a difficult time. For this reason we have set out below useful guidelines for coping with questions. These hints are based on common sense, but it helps to have a checklist.

GUIDELINES FOR ANSWERING QUESTIONS

We recommend you keep question-time to the end. The timing of questions is one of the factors that will help you to take control.

Questions come under the general heading of feedback in communication language. You will want feedback about the content of your presentation. Are there means other than questions of obtaining feedback? Well, there will be lots of feedback once implementation begins, but you are concerned now about what you have just presented. So ask some questions yourself, preferably open-ended questions that cannot be answered with a yes or no, unless that is what you need.

During the presentation your main concern is to get your big picture of the project across first. Questions out of turn can lead you into detail and off at a tangent. Note them, say you intend to discuss them later, otherwise you may never get to paint that big picture for your audience.

Ultimately, the question of when to have question time is a matter for you to decide. What is suitable? What is usual? What does your audience expect? Would you prefer points of clarity to be raised during the meeting?

Part of your preparation is anticipating opposition. Be aware, it is quite a natural reaction to react defensively when someone challenges or questions something in the plan. But try to avoid defensiveness. Can you anticipate some opposition or hostility you are likely to face in presenting your case?

Avoid putting other people down to make your point. Watch out for body language withdrawal signals. Some may withdraw by walking out. Others may simply become quiet but be equally withdrawn.

One result we have seen come out of quick answers to unexpected questions is over-commitment – that 'Yes, yes' reaction.

During question/discussion time encourage the group to come up with benefits that will accrue from the project.

You have completed your plan and presented it, and, congratulations, it has been accepted. All the work you have done in designing and developing the plan has been with this moment in mind. Implementation. Work begins on the project.

During planning you took the trouble to set up monitoring and control mechanisms. These will help you to easily adapt your plan as needed during implementation. The next chapter explains your role and the tools you will use in monitoring and controlling the project.

PART 4

*I*MPLEMENT AND AMEND THE PLAN

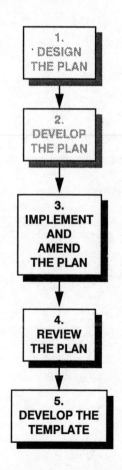

Checking the
progress

Nothing in Progression can rest on its original plan. We may as well think of rocking a grown man in the cradle of an infant.

Edmund Burke in a letter to W M Smith (29 Jan 1795)

THE PLANNER'S ROLE DURING IMPLEMENTATION

Work has begun on the project. The planner is responsible for submitting forecasts to management so that they can decide what measures, if any, should be taken to amend a situation. The information the planner submits alerts management to the need for change, e.g. the major change of rescheduling resources, and helps them to make their decisions. By providing different scenarios the planner makes it easier for the decision makers (see Chapter 15 'Problem solving and decision making').

The planner uses the logic diagram and other planning tools during implementation, namely the Gantt chart, resource histogram, timesheets, cash flow forecasts and 'S' curves. Whether the planner needs all of these tools depends on the needs of the project.

In short your role as planner in implementing and amending the plan is to:

- Gather information
- Collate information
- Provide information in different scenarios to feedback timely recommendations to management.

In the following case, scheduling had not been kept up to date during implementation.

CASE 5 – DON'T CROSS YOUR BRIDGES UNTIL . . .

The project was a pipe bridge in Cheshire, England – a modular construction to be used during the building of a chemical plant. The outcome of the project would be *'the bridge operational and maintained on the client site'*.

This project had four stages: design, construction, installation, maintenance.

Six different tradespeople worked on stage 2 of the project for three months during winter. The planning process took into account that time was critical and that there was a real possibility that the winter weather would hamper progress. Therefore they decided to build the module indoors. (No, we are not going to tell you that they omitted to plan on how to get it out of the building.) The structure was made of heavy steel, was 100 feet long and 12 feet high, and comprised walkways, numerous pipes and electrical cables, all in modular form to be brought to the site on a low loader.

Stage 2, construction of the bridge, went to plan. After the bridge builders celebrated this significant milestone, it was back to work on the first phase of stage 3, transportation of the module to the site. Loading was difficult but finally the bridge was ready to go.

Just as in their forward planning they had allowed for getting the structure out of the building in which they had worked, they had also discussed with Fred, the driver, the route the loader would take to the chemical site. Fred had said he would have to go the long way round because of a railway bridge that was too low to take the load. They added an extra half day to allow for this.

On the big day the chief engineer (the project manager) was absent from the site sorting out a conflict that had arisen on another project. Unbelievably, Fred, the driver, was away ill. A driver new to the area was substituted at the last minute. He took the short route...

Imagine this. The team of six in the now empty construction building awaiting the return of the chief engineer. When his burly frame fills the doorway they give him the bad news – serious damage to the structure. He relays this news to the client. 'What I want to know,' the client says, 'is whether it's going to delay the project?' The chief engineer does not know!

No matter how meticulously you plan, the wrong person in the wrong place at the wrong time is always a possibility. Could the accident have been avoided, and how? But we feel the main lesson to be learned from this case is this: if scheduling had been done and kept up to date on the logic diagram and the Gantt chart during implementation, the answer for the anxious client would have been readily accessible. Also, going a step further, by feeding this data into the schedule, they could have calculated the overall impact of the accident on the project objective (the bridge operational and maintained on the client site).

IMPLEMENTATION TOOLS

The main project planning and management tools are the logic diagram, the Gantt chart, the resource histogram and the 'S' curve.

At implementation, the purpose of these tools changes. In the beginning they are used to help set up and schedule the project work and resources. Now, during implementation, they will be used to measure actuals against estimates. That is to say, when the logic diagram, the Gantt chart, the resource histograms and the 'S' curve are finally signed off, the information they contain becomes the baseline against which actual progress and resource usage can be monitored. Monitoring enables you to make decisions concerning rescheduling or cancellation of the project where necessary. Use of the tools is an ongoing process, of course, not only for monitoring and controlling but for communicating changes and their effects.

Logic diagram

In designing your plan and then developing it, you used the logic diagram to identify the big picture of the summary plan, then the big picture of each chunk, and perhaps even at still lower detailed planning levels you, or the person delegated, used logic diagrams.

At all these levels, during implementation, the logic diagram is used to monitor and control and communicate.

Management, not involved in the details, manage the project at summary plan level (previously this logic diagram was an information generator), and the lower level logic diagrams are being used by the lower level members of the project team. As we said, the information they contain becomes a baseline against which what is actually happening at the various levels is measured (actuals against estimates).

In the past the Gantt chart was the main tool planners used to set out what, who, when and how much. Now there is a turnaround to designing and developing the plan in logic diagram form. We strongly support this because the logic diagram process begins with the end result of the project and allows you to identify the chunks of work that are needed to be completed to achieve the end result. It gives you a coordinated and logical sequence of events, the meaning of which is as clear as a picture – that is, the whole project can be seen at a glance.

Gantt chart

This shows tasks against time. It can also show costs against time. In fact, the planner can manipulate it to show any information measured against time.

If the planner is using computer technology in preparing a logic diagram, the computer will use the information from the logic diagram and produce a Gantt chart. The estimate of what may happen, as recorded on the logic diagram, becomes frozen on the Gantt chart. Writing immediately above this estimate, the planner records the actual (what is really happening) and then, immediately above that again, writes in the forecast, sometimes called the 'forecast to complete estimate'. At summary level this information is only for top management – for example, for resource breakdown, if needed. But, as we said, you can use this method of estimate, forecast and actual for all chunks of work.

The strength of the Gantt chart is seen during implementation. Its value is in its use in displaying the difference between the baseline estimate and actuals and also in showing schedule-to-complete forecasts (Figure 26).

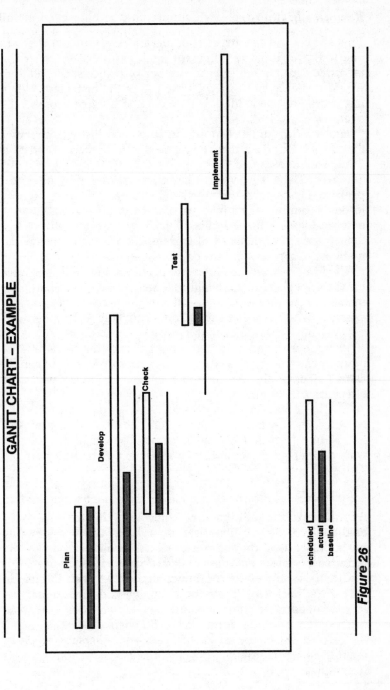

GANTT CHART – EXAMPLE

Plan

Develop

Check

Test

Implement

scheduled
actual
baseline

Figure 26

Resource histogram

This shows the resources (people and equipment) that are needed, and for how long, for each chunk of work. If the resources are shared over a number of projects, the planner would certainly be assisted by the use of the histogram. When resources are overloaded, resource smoothing can correct the overload.

Figure 27(a) (unlevelled and unsmoothed histogram) shows that days 1, 3 and 5 are not being used to full capacity, and days 2 and 4 are in overload.

Figure 27(b) (smoothed histogram) shows how overload peaks in days 2 and 4 are smoothed by using some spare capacity in day 3, putting day 5 into overload by two hours and paying overtime, leaving day 1 as it is. The date is not extended.

In Figure 27(c) (levelled histogram) there is no overtime and no filling of capacity, but the date is extended.

The importance of the histogram is that it highlights resource conflicts not shown on the logic diagram or the Gantt chart. This makes it an effective aid to negotiation and decision making, for example when you can show from the histogram where overload occurs and its effect on the project.

With some project management computer software the planner can develop 'what if... ?' scenarios by keying in certain assumptions on the logic diagram and seeing immediately their effects on the resource histogram.

Say the planner feeds in data concerning non-availability of a resource, they would see the resulting delays and/or overloading. Figures 27(b) and 27(c) are examples of some of the different ways of dealing with resource conflict using resource histograms.

Timesheets

Information for monitoring and controlling the project is gathered and recorded on timesheets on a daily, weekly or monthly basis depending on the needs of the project. It states the resource (people or equipment) and the period (see Figure 28).

Original estimates are not shown on the timesheet. The reason is that the staff should now be basing their estimates (of how long is needed to complete, and what it will cost) on what actually remains to be done – *not on the original estimates*.

Figure 29 shows the total actual hours or dollars for people or equipment per chunk of work plus the estimates and forecasts to complete.

RESOURCE HISTOGRAM – UNLEVELLED, UNSMOOTHED

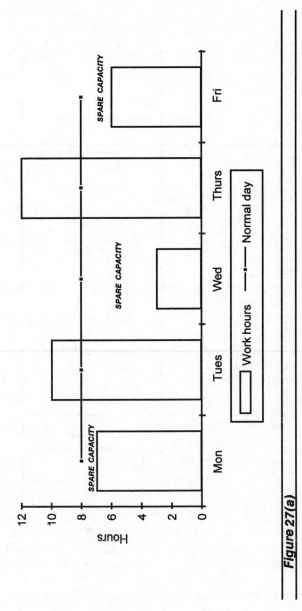

Figure 27(a)

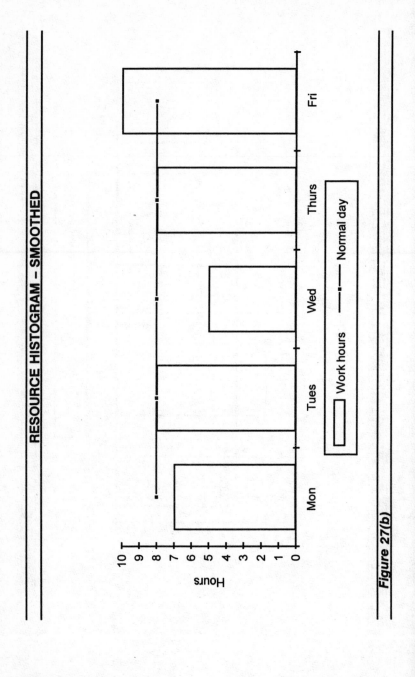

Figure 27(b)

RESOURCE HISTOGRAM – LEVELLED

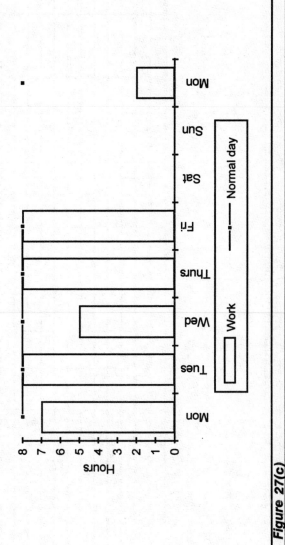

Figure 27(c)

113

TIMESHEET – SAMPLE

Resource name:..........................

Week ending:..........................

Project code:..........................

TASK DESCRIPTION	TASK CODE	M	T	W	TH	F	S	S	Total for period	Estimate to complete	Actual start	Actual finish

signed:..........................

Figure 28

114

ESTIMATES, ACTUALS, FORECASTS TO COMPLETE (in hours or cost)

Task name	Estimate	Actual	Forecast to complete
Catalogue printed	100	50	90

Figure 29

'S' curve

The planner can use information from the timesheets to create an 'S' curve chart. An 'S' curve is a control tool which shows your forecasts against your baseline estimates. It gives you a picture of what the overall impact is likely to be if you continue along the lines of the forecast. Where marked differences between the baseline and the forecast occur, people such as the project manager can determine why this is happening and decide what has to be done to bring the forecast back to the baseline.

You can see from Figure 30 that the 'S' curve is about looking forward (not backwards). It is about forecasting.

Summary

Your role as planner during implementation is to:

- Gather information, collate it, use it to provide scenarios for decision making
- Use implementation tools to measure actuals against estimates
- Reschedule work and resources as necessary
- Let people know of changes affecting them.

Depending on the complexity and risk factors relating to your project, your role as planner may end with completion of the project documentation. We are assuming you are still with the project. In the next chapter we cover reviewing the plan and making a template.

'S' CURVE – EXAMPLE

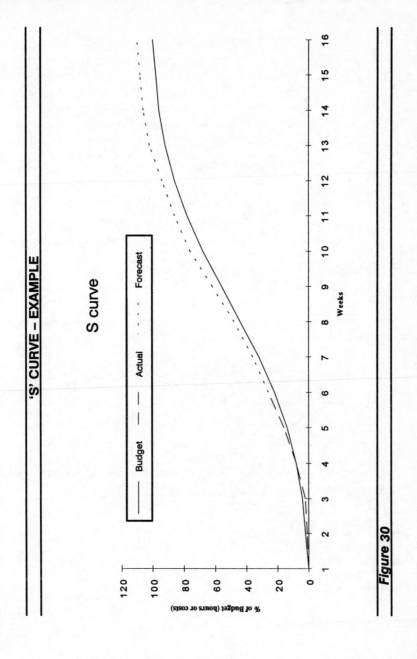

S curve

Figure 30

117

*A*ssessing for the future

REVIEW THE PLAN AND DEVELOP THE TEMPLATE

Once the project has been completed and the project vision, in its original form or amended, is in place, you review the plan. What can we learn from what we did? What could we have done better? The answers form the basis of a template you will prepare for future similar projects.

Review the plan

Reviewing is a process by which we identify the strengths and weaknesses of the plan. This is particularly valuable where similar projects are likely to be undertaken in the future. With the future in mind, the aim of the review is to develop a template or to amend an existing one.

Develop the template

'Template' is a word in common usage today. Only the brave ask what it means.

Before defining it, let us look at what a template does in terms of project management, particularly in terms of planning.

The very first time a project was planned in your organization, most probably you started from scratch. If, as an experienced project worker, you are still starting each project at square one, unless your projects are one-offs, you are not benefiting from your knowledge of what has worked in the past.

A template serves as a guide for similar projects. It is an outline, an infrastructure, a prototype, a model. It is developed from the information you garner in reviewing the plan. After any project, the question must be asked: 'Is our organization likely to do anything like this again?' If the answer is 'Yes', then the information that surfaces from the review is a worthwhile resource, particularly if the project under review was a complex, time-consuming, expensive operation. Future possible ben efits are obvious – short cuts and money-savers. The differences that occurred between what was planned and what actually happened can be used to develop or fine tune a planning template. You might even be able to market your template.

So, a template is a mould, if we use the dictionary definition, 'a mould used as a guide in shaping', a pattern that adapts easily. You may have seen computer programs that allow you to set up templates for memos, letters, architectural designs, that sort of thing. We used a template for this book based on our previous publication, *A Practical Guide to Project Management*.

Templates consist of:

- Logic diagram at summary level
- Detailed sub-set plans supported by Gantt charts
- Formats for your working documents.

When the group of educators in the following case study became deeply involved in the planning process already in place to integrate private schools into the state system, they reviewed the integration process and developed a template which resulted in dramatic improvement in the procedure.

CASE 6 – INTEGRATION OF SCHOOLS

Chuck, Ian and Brian form a team that has streamlined the process of integration of private schools into the New Zealand state education system. These specialists bring to the job their in-depth knowledge of the education system and of the Private Schools Conditional Integration Act 1975 and its requirements. Using project planning techniques they developed a standard planning template. The action sheet that forms part of the template is shown in Figure 31.

Historical background of the project

Since 1975, some 400 private schools in New Zealand have integrated with the state system. In the mid-seventies, private schools were facing increasing financial hardship. Some were going under. The state system could not absorb the influx of pupils if the private school system collapsed. The Private Schools Integration Act 1975 was originally brought in to assist schools in financial difficulty. Under the Act, funding was for operational and property costs to ensure the schools ran to a set standard. Then and now, legislation preserves the specific character of the school, for example, philosophical or religious. Ownership of the school land and buildings remains with the proprietor.

The specialist school integration project team

Chuck specializes in school property, is responsible for assessment of the condition of lands and buildings, decides what is needed to bring it to the standard required by the state, receives reports from sub-contractors concerning building specifications (fire, electrical, mechanical, health, gas, structure, roofing), and architectural drawings showing all services.

Ian specializes in school operations, is responsible for collecting information concerning curriculum, teaching methods, number of teachers, salaries, roll information and prediction – anything to do with the overall running of the school. He also prepares the legal documentation.

Brian, architect, is responsible to Chuck for as-built drawings.

The process of integration

When the application for integration is received from the school, the specialists pay an initial visit to assess the situation. The assessment covers two main areas: property and operations. Under the Act, the proprietor must own the land and buildings.

Following the assessment, the team send a submission to the school advising them of the proceedings, the estimated time-frames and the cost.

On receipt of the submission based on the assessment, if the

TEMPLATE – EXAMPLE ACTION SHEET – Preliminary board/school meeting

Person	Hrs.	Code	Task title	Date due	Actioned
		1.1	PROPERTY		
		1.1.1	Check site plan and drawings		
		1.1.2	Prepare site plan and line drawings		
		1.1.2.1	Prepare draft schedules		
		1.1.3	Obtain working drawings		
		1.1.4	Obtain heat, light and water accounts		
		1.1.5	Obtain reports: • Roofing • Structural • Electrical • Mechanical • Fire • Council permits • MOE registration		

Figure 31

school wishes to proceed with the application, the specialist project team presents a submission to the Ministry of Education on behalf of the school.

The submission contains a detailed maintenance schedule showing what maintenance is required, with the work required spread over a negotiated time. Maintenance relating to health and safety must be done immediately. Operational requirements are also included in the submission.

Then, based on the information in the submission, the interested parties, that is, the Ministry, the school representatives and the specialist project team, meet to negotiate the level of funding. The negotiations proceed, special character is agreed, a maximum standard is set, a date is set for integration. The final documents are signed.

The specialist team reviews the integration process

The first question the team asked was, 'Why is this process taking so long – four years from application for integration to the realization?' Where were the hold-ups?

Their analysis of the process showed that the major hold-ups were mainly flaws in communication – information was not always sufficiently clear, concise, complete or even correct. What resulted was a lot of backward and forward movement of the same documents while people sought clarification. Other important factors that slowed up the integration process included political elections and delays caused by the school proprietors' failure to provide proof of ownership of land and buildings. In this regard, also, difficulties arose with shared ownership. There was also the vital question of defining the special character of the private school. With the Catholic schools, special character was easily defined. Some schools, however, were difficult to define – Montessori, for example – and required separate negotiations.

The specialist team draws up the template

Armed with the results of their analysis, they refined the integration process and developed a template. To save time in discussion, the specialist team ensured that everyone in attendance at all meetings was thoroughly briefed – the team itself, sub-contractors, the school proprietors, as well as Ministry of Education officials.

Communication became a top priority for which the specialists took responsibility. They saw to it that, as well as being briefed, everyone understood what was expected of them. In addition, leaving nothing to chance, when the specialists made submissions to the Ministry on behalf of the schools, they supplemented their written reports with face-to-face discussion of the contents and any possible issues, thereby ensuring that issues were dealt with without delay and before negotiation meetings took place. Because of this, the negotiation meetings took only two hours. At the meetings, after a brief full session, the group split into two, each smaller group discussing either property or operations. The series of meetings ended with both groups coming together to sign the contracts.

Using this template, the procedure that previously took up to four years can now be accomplished in approximately six months.

Summary

In reviewing the plan, you:

- Identify the strengths and weaknesses of the plan
- Decide whether to develop a template or to amend an existing one.

In developing the template, you:

- Pass on to others the benefit of your knowledge
- Prepare an outline of a project plan, a pattern that adapts easily for future use on similar projects.

This completes the planning process. You may have an interest in marketing planning, and in problem solving and decision making in planning, which we touch on in the next chapters.

MARKETING, PROBLEM SOLVING, BRAINSTORMING, DATA MODELLING

CHAPTER | **M**arketing

14 | planning

Marketing is anything but an exact science, and the marketing planning process is slightly different from most other project planning. We find it helpful to use the planning principles in this book in conjunction with the marketing matrices set out below.

MARKETING PLANNING MATRICES

The matrices were published in his book *Market-led Strategic Change* (Oxford: Butterworth-Heinemann, 1993) by Professor Nigel Piercy of Cardiff Business School, University of Wales, who has kindly given us permission to include them here.

Figure 32(a) is a map or graph on which students plotted the figures from each of the four matrices that follow (Figures 32(b)–(e)). It measures the probability of events occurring (low to high), and their effect on the condom industry (excellent to disastrous).

We use the next case study to show how the matrices were used on a marketing planning assignment given to students on an MBA course in 1987.

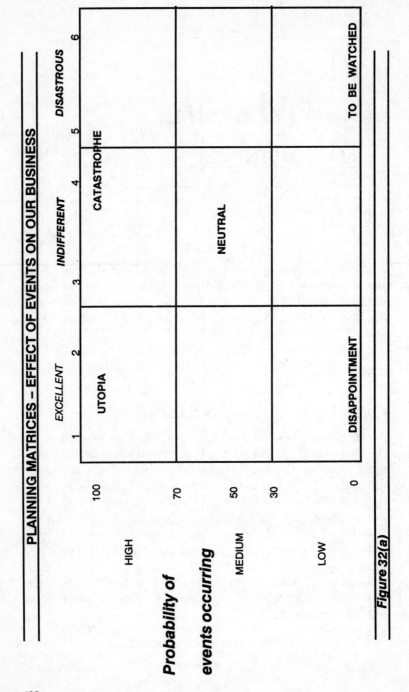

PLANNING MATRICES – EFFECT OF EVENTS ON OUR BUSINESS

Probability of events occurring

Figure 32(a)

PLANNING MATRICES – POLITICAL ENVIRONMENT

Major events	Specific impacts of the event on the business	Effect of the event on our business (Score 1 to 7)	Probability of the event occurring (Score 0 to 100)
P1	. . .		
P2	. . .		
P3	. . .		
P4	. . .		

Figure 32(b)

PLANNING MATRICES – TECHNOLOGICAL ENVIRONMENT

Major events	Specific impacts of the event on the business	Effect of the event on our business (Score 1 to 7)	Probability of the event occurring (Score 0 to 100)
T1	. . .		
T2	. . .		
T3	. . .		
T4	. . .		

Figure 32(c)

PLANNING MATRICES – SOCIAL ENVIRONMENT

Major events	Specific impacts of the event on the business	Effect of the event on our business (Score 1 to 7)	Probability of the event occurring (Score 0 to 100)
S1	. . .		
S2	. . .		
S3	. . .		
S4	. . .		

Figure 32(d)

PLANNING MATRICES – ECONOMIC ENVIRONMENT

Major events	Specific impacts of the event on the business	Effect of the event on our business (Score 1 to 7)	Probability of the event occurring (Score 0 to 100)
E1	. . .		
E2	. . .		
E3	. . .		
E4	. . .		

Figure 32(e)

CASE 7 – THE STUDENTS PUT THEORY INTO PRACTICE

The assignment was to carry out an environmental scan of the condom industry in the United Kingdom over the next three years using the attached matrices as guidelines.

The students understood that 'strategy' could be compared with what you see from a plane at 20,000 feet – the macro picture, the global view. Thinking strategically, the students clarified their mission and success criteria, then asked themselves what they had to do to reach these objectives. 'Big picture' objectives included gathering marketing information about environmental events that could affect the whole contraceptive industry. As well, the students needed to forecast and track trends and attitudes over the three-year period. Their main success criterion at the end of three years would be the accuracy of their forecasts concerning the condom industry.

Next, the detailed programme of action (the micro view) would include obtaining information on the marketing mix of all contraceptive products and the segmentation and positioning in the market of the condom. Armed with market information from their research, they used matrices to measure effect on the industry of specified environmental events. These events fell into two groups.

In the first, or wider, group, the issues included factors that impacted on society as a whole (demographic trends, and political, cultural, economic, technological, economic factors). In the next, the students reviewed in detail the condom industry relative to the contraceptive industry, considering such things as market size, demand, competitors, suppliers, technological innovations and distribution. They used the matrix headed 'Effect of the events on our business' to do a SWOT analysis, identifying strengths and weaknesses within the industry to measure against environmental opportunities and threats. For example, the fact that the condom was not only a readily obtainable contraceptive but an effective protection against sexually transmitted diseases was a strength. A threat was the possible discovery of a miracle drug that was both a protection against disease and a contraceptive.

Here is an example of how the matrices could be used in relation to this case study. Say the major event was that the public learned that prolonged use of the contraceptive pill endangered health, the specific impact on the condom business would be likely to be favourable, resulting in increased sales.

Using the diagrams the planner would then consider the probability of that event occurring. Other major events could be:

- War (political): The outcome would be, perhaps, free distribution to the military by the government
- Widespread unemployment (economic): The outcome could be that the cost put the product financially beyond the reach of many people.

In 1987 when the study took place, the condom industry was in decline. As events turned out, the incidence of AIDS increased dramatically during the study and the study assumed a new importance. Its results far exceeded expectations and were used commercially.

In Chapter 1, Case 1 (Dreamcream Biscuits takes the cake) focused on how a company lost and regained its market share. At first glance you might think that in the following study the topic is similar. In addition, however, to the question of market share, we invite you to identify the traps Pulsar Products Ltd fell into. The names are fictitious. We analyse the case at the end.

CASE 8 – PULSAR LTD MISSES A BEAT

The computer software market is fiercely competitive. At the time, Sim-tec Ltd has the bulk of the market with its easy-to-use products.

Pulsar Products Ltd wants a bigger share of the market. Management decide to target one particular Sim-tec product. The aggressive strategy they devise has one objective: to take away Sim-tec's market share.

In their advertising campaign they invite the owners of Sim-tec's lightweight product to trade it in: 'Pulsar Products will take it off your hands and replace it with our own superior heavier duty product for approximately one quarter of our product's usual retail price.'

The strategy works. Pulsar floods the market with their product.

In the meantime, Sim-tec Ltd is slowly getting ready for retaliatory action. Using the same aggressive tactics as Pulsar Products they will go further. It takes them twelve months, but then they hit back with a clever strategy of their own.

During that year of preparation they analyse the competition's product and their own. They confirm that Pulsar's heavy-duty package is hard to use. The analysis also reveals a flaw in their own product which they correct. In effect, they keep their product's simplicity, but add new benefits.

When Sim-tec Ltd advertise their lighter duty product as 'user-friendly with new added features', the strategy works again. They win back their lost customers.

Now let us analyse Case 8. As we see it, Pulsar Products Ltd erred by omission. They did not take their planning process and thinking far enough. They failed to consider the impact their gaining Sim-tec Ltd's market would have on both their competitor and the public.

An obvious question was: 'What is Sim-tec likely to do in return?' But more pressing than that, thinking ahead could have raised the question about the possible reaction of Pulsar's new customers to the new heavy-duty computer package. Pulsar might have identified what was likely to happen and what did in fact happen as soon as they had taken in Sim-tec's product and distributed their own: the consumers jammed their telephone lines, asking 'How does it work?' They were used to an easy-to-use package. They could not use the new one. It was too hard.

Pulsar Products Ltd hit the wrong target: people who did not need heavy-duty software and who could not use it. They saturated the market with a technical product designed for heavy-duty users. A SWOT analysis would have identified a weakness in their product (it was not user-friendly); it would also have identified an opportunity (a training facility for new users). In creating a demand for the product on the one hand, and on the other hand failing to support the novices who rang up ('How do you use this?'), they damaged their image and left the market wide open for Sim-tec to come back with their user-friendly product.

Because of their tunnel vision, Pulsar Products Ltd lost not only credibility and business, but an opportunity in a niche market, namely, training.

Postscript: did you wonder why it took Sim-tec Ltd a whole

year to hit back? Do they too need to look further ahead in their strategic planning?

Summary

In planning marketing, you:

- Use matrices to scan the environment and predict trends
- Use the matrices to consider impacts on competitors, the public, your own company, etc.

*P*roblem solving
and decision making

PROBLEM SOLVING AND DECISION MAKING
AS PART OF THE PLANNING PROCESS

A problem can be seen as an opportunity to enhance an organization. Projects are often conceived as solutions to problems. Problem solving and decision making continue through the life cycle of projects.

The problem-solving and decision-making process begins with identifying the problem and collecting information. The problem can then be more closely defined and the benefits of change analysed and decisions made. If there are several possible solutions, the planner determines what are likely to be the most beneficial, successful, costly. A competent planner will devise scenarios that will aid decision making. Sometimes this means in-depth planning. It may even be necessary to design and develop a detailed solution to the problem in the form of a project.

Often problems occur within a project. The following is such a case. It illustrates how problem solving and decision making enabled an organization to develop a plan that helped ensure a satisfactory outcome.

CASE 9 – FIRST CAPTURE THE VISION, THEN DEVELOP THE PLAN

The organization is being streamlined. Management's desired outcome is increased productivity. The Human Resources Unit is brought in. The roles of two types of technicians will have to be combined; it will be necessary to train the technicians and to get their agreement about their new employment contracts.

It is this brief that management presents to the Human Resource Unit (HRU) who are required to develop the plan, establish its feasibility and then present it to management for approval.

HRU brings in a consultant to develop the high-level summary plan and the detailed working plans.

First, discussions take place between the consultant and the core team which clarify the main issue: differences between management's perspective and HRU's perspective of the final output. In organizations generally, this gap in perspective between senior management and other management levels is not uncommon.

In this case, on the one hand HRU perceive the goal as 'technicians' roles changed', with the major conflicts likely to be in the area of industrial relations: the changing function of the worker, the renegotiation of contracts. On the other hand, senior management's desired overall output is 'productivity increased'.

The consultant's immediate objective in solving this problem is to ensure that management, HRU and everyone affected by the planning has the same vision, i.e. 'productivity increased'. Now the project does not end with the implementation of the combined technician roles. Who, the consultant asks, is going to *put in place and be responsible for the system that is needed to assess the impact on productivity.*

The core team agrees to recommend that HRU plan for and manage this extra stage.

HRU planners then identify the major chunks of work needed and develop a logic diagram, e.g. new functions and responsibilities accepted by the technicians; contracts negotiated; technicians trained; technicians operating in new roles; productivity monitoring systems in place; productivity and new roles reviewed.

Communication strategy was also included to deal with uncertainty regarding contracts and potential contract negotiation conflict. A communication strategy would add cost to the project and would take longer at the beginning. So management were at first against the idea. The core team felt the communication strategy was critical and used logic diagram scenarios to show how it would speed up the project during negotiations, and in the long run save money, and possibly face.

The above case illustrates the use of logic diagram scenarios in decision making. Problem solving and decision matrices as shown in Figure 33 have proved their value too in weighing up options and making decisions.

BRAINSTORMING AND MINDMAPPING

In Chapter 2 'visionary brainstorming' was the method by which we identified chunks of work needed for the project. In brainstorming, the whole team calls out their ideas and the planner comes up with a haphazard list which is later put into logical order. That is one recognized technique.

Another method used for planning, problem solving, structuring, brainstorming and for note taking is called 'mind mapping'. In all these activities we often tend to write in lists. Our brain, however, works with key concepts in an interlinked and integrated manner. Tony Buzan, in his book, *Use Your Head*, makes the point that, that being so, 'our notes and our word relations should in many instances be structured in this way rather than in traditional 'lines''. Have a look at the mind map in Figure 34. At first glance it may look disorderly. It is in fact more structured and logically built up than an ordinary list. It saved time for the teacher in charge of planning the rugby tournament. You can see how quickly the teacher arrived at the overview and how readily sub-sets flowed from the main ideas. All this information will transfer easily to logic diagrams (summary plan and sub-sets).

What we particularly like about a completed mind-mapping diagram is how the important ideas leap to the eye from near the centre and how clear it is that the less important are the ones furthest from the centre. The open-ended nature of the pattern adds to the creativity. The brain makes new connections and sub-chunks of work emerge in greater depth. Look at the diagram again and see how it allows for the easy addition of new information.

DECISION MATRIX

	Benefits	Issues	
Option 1.			
Option 2.			
Option 3.			

Figure 33

MINDMAP - EXAMPLE

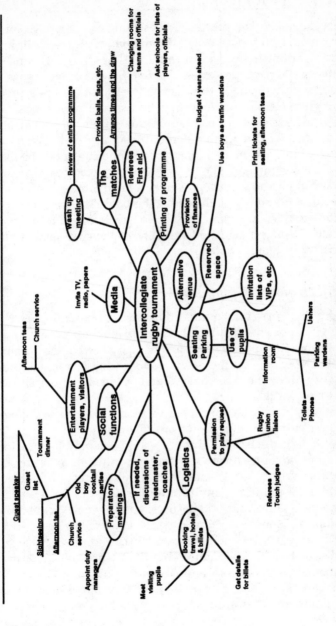

Figure 34

DATA MODELLING

Data modelling is a process for designing computer systems. A data model prescribes how information is gathered within an organization. It shows information flows and relationships between data and processes. The free-flowing language we are used to in dialogue with other people is not always a precise enough mode of communicating. Data modelling is precise. It is a foundation stone of communication within an organization and formally documents communication flows. We have a two-fold purpose in mentioning data modelling here. The first is that we recommend that, if you are not already aware of this powerful planning concept, you become informed about it. We provide a reading list at the end of this book. The second purpose is to show you, in Figure 35, how we have used the technique to produce a project data model that shows the vital elements to be considered in project planning.

Vital elements of planning

A group of project planners addressed the question, What are the vital elements that make up the planning process? Using a brainstorming approach, the following list is what they came up with. Depending on the nature of your project, you will probably use all of them to some degree. Consider using this as a planning checklist.

Stages; phases; levels; chunks (of work); tasks; logic sequence; success criteria; priority; problem solving; options (solutions to problems); decision points; unknowns; paths; durations; recommendations; reviews; scenarios; control mechanisms; integration; critical areas; timeframe; milestones; budget; risk; estimates; planning environment; roles; quality standards (IS09000); performance measures; contingencies; constraints; communication; vision; SWOT (strengths; weaknesses; opportunities; threats); feasibility; impact; links and effects; structure; skills; materials; equipment; objectives; approvals; milestones presentation format (oral and written).

Figure 35 (project data model) was developed from the vital elements. It sets out the scope of your plan and suggests the wide range of information you require in setting up, managing and winding up a project.

Using our planning approach you can quickly and easily

PROJECT DATA MODEL

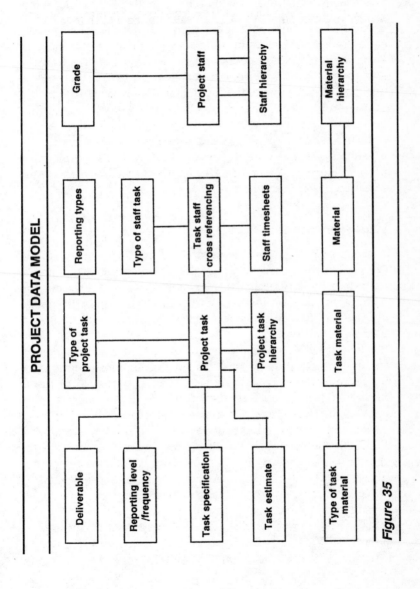

Figure 35

143

identify the main entities of a project that fall within these categories.

At all stages of your planning, see the plan as a means of coordinating, not controlling. Your plan is not a crystal ball that tells you exactly when events will occur. It is the framework within which you coordinate work and test the impact of changes.

*A*fterword

You can plan a project to death. You can underplan. If you do the latter then hour after costly hour will be spent in crisis management.

Our hope is that what we have put in this book will help planners find their optimal level of planning effort for each project.

Recommended reading

Albert, K J (1980) *Handbook of Business Problem Solving*, McGraw-Hill.

Bass, J (1989) *The Executive Guide to Operational Planning*, Morrissey Below Acomb.

Burton, C and Michael, N (1992) *A Practical Guide to Project Management*, Kogan Page.

Gane, C and Sarson, T (1979) *Structured Systems Analysis and Design*, Prentice-Hall, New Jersey.

Higgins, J C (1985) *Computer-Based Planning Systems*, Edward Arnold Ltd.

Kerzner, H (1984) *Project Management. A Systems Approach to Planning, Scheduling, and Controlling*, second edition, Van Nostrand Reinhold.

Kindler, H S (1991) *Risk Taking*, Kogan Page.

Martin (1982) *Strategic Data-Planning Methodologies*, Prentice Hall.

Mackenzie, A (1990) *The Time Trap*, The Business Library.

Piercy, N (1992) *Market-led Strategic Change*, Butterworth-Heinemann.

Pokras, S (1990) *Systematic Problem Solving and Decision Making*, Kogan Page.

Sheffield, J and Meyer, M D (1990) *New Zealand Cases in Information Systems*, Pagination Publishers.

Tsichritzis, L (1982) *Data Models*, Prentice Hall.

Index